What people are saying about Beautiful Feet...

"Danny's enthusiasm and energy for evangelism has always been an example to me. His simple style and interesting insights make this a quick and enjoyable read—like watching an expert fisherman bring in the 'big one.' My fire for personal evangelism has been rekindled again."

Pastor Bob Coy
Calvary Chapel Fort Lauderdale

"You hold in your hands a powerful tool in learning how to better share your faith. **Beautiful Feet** is Danny Lehmann's latest book on reaching others with the Gospel. Danny is one of modern evangelism's most effective communicators and a personal friend of mine."

"The principles he shares in this book come from years of Bible study and Danny's amazing stories of reaching out with the Gospel. I am confident your witness for Jesus will be stronger as a result of reading this book. I highly recommend it."

Greg Laurie
Pastor & Evangelist, Harvest Christian Fellowship

"Danny Lehmann has the true gift of evangelism. American television portrays an evangelist as a superstar and a celebrity. Other than Dr. Billy Graham, few show that the work of evangelism includes discipleship. Danny has inspired thousands worldwide to follow Jesus in winning souls. Not only is he a soul winner, but the fruit of his ministry has multiplied disciples for Jesus Christ who are also soul winners. I recommend **Beautiful Feet** to the reader—you will be inspired."

Pastor Mike MacIntosh
Horizon Christian Fellowship

What people are saying about Beautiful Feet...

"If ever there was a man who practiced what he preached, it's Danny Lehmann. I've known him up close and personal, and what he writes about he is actively doing."

"*Beautiful Feet* is a must for new believers, to infuse evangelism into their spiritual DNA right from the start. And it's a necessity for older believers too who may have fallen out of the habit of sharing their faith."

Pastor Bill Stonebraker
Calvary Chapel of Honolulu

"Danny Lehmann is one of the few brothers in Christ that I have personally met and spent time with who constantly carries an authentic and sincere passion to reach people for Jesus Christ. His writings are easy to follow, intensely practical, and are backed up by his life. Danny Lehmann practices what he preaches! I am sure that you will be greatly challenged and helped by *Beautiful Feet*."

K. P. Yohannan
President, Gospel for Asia

OTHER BOOKS BY DANNY LEHMANN

Bringin' 'Em Back Alive
Before You Hit The Wall
Stoked

Beautiful Feet
Steps to a Lifestyle of Evangelism

by Danny Lehmann
with Scott Tomkins

How beautiful ... are the feet of those who
bring good news ...who proclaim salvation.
—Isaiah 52:7, NIV

Calvary Chapel Publishing
Santa Ana, California

Beautiful Feet

<u>Dedication</u>

To those with "Beautiful Feet" who GO.
To those who have yet to hear.

TABLE OF CONTENTS

Foreword xi

Acknowledgements xiii

Section I-The *MESSENGERS* of the Good News 1

    Chapter 1- Jesus - Our Role Model of Evangelism 7

    Chapter 2- Keep it Simple 13

             (Profile: Philip)

    Chapter 3- Armed with Supernatural Power 19

             (Profile: Peter)

    Chapter 4- The Seeds of Sacrifice 31

             (Profile: Stephen)

    Chapter 5- Spirit-Led Strategies 37

             (Profile: Paul)

Section II-The *MESSAGE* of the Good News 49

    Chapter 6- True Truth 51

    Chapter 7- The First Word of the Gospel 59

    Chapter 8- The Good News in Person 65

    Chapter 9- Saving Faith 71

    Chapter 10- Our Future Home 79

Section III-The *MOTIVES* for Sharing the Good News 87

    Chapter 11- Love 89

    Chapter 12- Lordship 97

    Chapter 13- The Lostness of the Lost 103

    Chapter 14- The Last Days 109

    Chapter 15- Abundant Life 117

Table of Contents cont.

Section IV-The *METHODS* of Sharing the Good News...... 125

    Chapter 16- Pre-Evangelism 129

    Chapter 17- Presence Evangelism 137

    Chapter 18- Proclamation Evangelism 145

    Chapter 19- Persuasion Evangelism 157

    Chapter 20- Propagation Evangelism 165

Appendix I-The Top Ten Questions Non-Christians Ask About the Gospel 175

Appendix II-Street Jesus 187

Appendix III-The Top Ten Overstatements Made About Evangelism.. 193

Appendix IV-Recommended Reading 197

Appendix V-100 Reasons We Should Evangelize the World 199

Endnotes... 205

FOREWORD

We are called by Christ to be His witnesses to the whole world. Paul, in his letter to the Romans, asked, "How…shall they call on Him in whom they have not believed? And how shall they believe in Him of whom they have not heard?" He then quoted from the prophet Isaiah, "How beautiful are the feet of them that preach the Gospel of peace, and bring glad tidings of good things!" I do not know of anyone today who is more qualified to write on the subject of how to bring glad tidings of good things to others than Danny Lehmann. He does not share from theory, but from personal experience.

In his book, *Beautiful Feet, Steps to a Lifestyle of Evangelism*, Danny leads us from Biblical examples of personal evangelism to the actual message of hope that we have to bring to a dying world. He then gives us the great incentives to share our message, as well as practical suggestions on how to share.

The Apostle Paul felt that it was his obligation to share the good news of the risen Christ to the whole world. He said that he was a debtor to all men and was not ashamed of the Gospel of Jesus Christ, "…for it is the power of God to salvation for everyone who believes." Many an earnest Christian would like to share their faith with others, but feel they lack the skills to do so. This book will not only inspire and challenge you to share your faith with others, but will give you practical advice on how to bring others to a saving faith in Jesus Christ. This book is a must-read for every Christian who longs for beautiful feet.

Pastor Chuck Smith
Calvary Chapel of Costa Mesa

ACKNOWLEDGEMENTS

Special thanks to:

Scott Tomkins for helping me "write the vision and make it plain..."

Stephanie Headley for typing (and re-typing) the manuscript.

Romy Godding for wielding her editing scissors with compassion.

Pastors Bill Stonebraker, Chuck Smith, Garry Ansdell, and Mark Buckley for teaching, counsel, and inspiration.

Evangelists Greg Laurie, Mike MacIntosh, Raul Ries, Ray Comfort, Robert Coleman, and Michael Green for stoking the evangelistic fire in my heart.

Mission Leaders Loren Cunningham, Jim Stier, George Verwer, and K.P. Yohannan for their vision of the "Big Picture."

The Lehmanns: Linda, Daniel, Esther, and David for everything.

SECTION I

The Messengers of the Good News

Plop! The neatly bundled packet of "Living Water" Gospel tracts landed right in my lap as I lay stretched out on the overstuffed couch at Shekinah House, a Christian rehabilitation center near Santa Cruz, California. "Get up, Danny! We're going witnessing," announced my friend and mentor, Homer Rivera. "You've been saved for over a month now, and it's time for you to start learning how to win souls."

I was less than enthusiastic, but I slowly rose from the sofa, bundled my hair in a ponytail, and walked out with Homer for my first experience at street witnessing. I was trembling with fear by the time we had our first encounter. My friend would walk up to total strangers, and with a winning smile and a genuine concern for their eternal destiny, he would press a tract into their hand and engage them in conversation.

After an hour or so of tagging along, Homer finally turned to me and said the words I knew were coming: "Now it's your turn." After a couple of rejections, a young surfer guy not only took my Gospel tract, but looked me in the eye to ask what it was about. I froze and became speechless. Thankfully, Homer took over the conversation and told the young man about the love of Jesus.

Eventually my speech instrument thawed from its freeze, and I started telling people what God had done for me and what He could do for them. Since that experience, I have gone witnessing hundreds of times, have passed out tens of thousands of Gospel tracts, and have had the thrill of seeing hundreds of people give their lives to Jesus Christ. Evangelism is now an important part of my everyday life, and it comes as natural to me now as it did then to my friend Homer.

With or without tracts, on the street or off, I hope it will soon be an everyday part of your life too. I believe there is no more important mission for a believer than to introduce others to Jesus Christ. C.H. Spurgeon, known as the Prince of Preachers, said, "Soulwinning is the chief business of the Christian minister; indeed it should be the main pursuit of every true believer."[1] Nothing is more fulfilling than seeing someone you've led to the Lord be transformed by His love and grace.

Before we go any further, let me ask you a question—how did you come to know the Lord? If you're like nine out of ten Christians, a caring friend, co-worker, or family member led you to Christ.[2]

Now consider another question: how many people have you personally led to Christ? Most likely, the answer is none. Surveys show that nearly nine out of ten professing Christians have never led a soul to Jesus.[3]

These figures reveal just how powerful an influence we can have in leading people to the Lord and how little we use that power. What if the 10 percent figure of those bringing in the harvest rose to 20 percent? 30? 50? Just imagine what could happen if *all* sincere Christians made it a high priority to tell their friends, neighbors, and co-workers about Jesus. In just a short time, the whole world could be radically changed.

The goal of this book is to radically change the world—through people just like you. It teaches practical skills that make it easy to present the Gospel. It shows how to develop a *lifestyle* of personal evangelism where you work, live, and play. It examines the who (messenger), what (message), why (motives), and how (methods) of our outreach to the world. And it also helps you look beyond your present sphere of influence to a world God loves, a world in desperate need of a Savior.

I want to spark in you and every other reader of this book a passion for personal evangelism. Whether or not you realize it, God has a call on your life. He wants to involve you in His great plan to take His good news to a lost world that desperately needs to be found.

You begin by reaching out to those closest to you—family, friends, neighbors, and co-workers. But by no means do you stop there. God is calling out a generation of radical, all-for-Jesus believers who will take up Christ's commission to "go…and make disciples of all the nations" (Matthew 28:19).

Putting 'Feet' to Our Faith

The most important single characteristic of a committed Christian is a willingness to "put feet" to his or her faith in obedience to God—to go where He leads for sake of the Gospel.

GO stands out as the "biggest little word in the Bible." It is listed 1,492 times in the Scripture and is the defining mission of some of the Bible's greatest men and women. God told Abraham to *go* into an unknown land that He would show him. He told Moses to *go* and lead His people into the Promised Land. He told Noah to *go* and build an ark (He even told him to use "*go*"-pher wood; sorry, I couldn't resist!). He told the Apostle Paul to *go* and proclaim the good news to the Gentiles. And He commissioned believers of every age to *go* into all the world and preach the Gospel (see Mark 16:15).

Something beautiful happens when we obey the Lord and *go*. Because of the Holy Spirit's presence within us, we bring that redemptive spirit of Jesus Christ to every place we set foot. No wonder Isaiah declared,

> How beautiful on the mountains are the feet of those who bring good news, who proclaim peace, who bring good tidings, who proclaim salvation, who say to Zion, "Your God reigns!"
>
> —Isaiah 52:7, NIV

You may have never considered your feet beautiful. You may even consider them downright ugly. You may have flat feet, fat feet, skinny feet, or athletic feet. You may be knock-kneed, pigeon-toed, or club-footed. But when you use your feet for walking out God's will, they become beautiful instruments of salvation. They are a beautifully crafted, precise combination of 26 bones and a network of supporting tendons, tissues, ligaments, and blood vessels that are your primary means of obeying Jesus' command to *go*. 'Go' means a change of location. In our case, it's to take the Gospel to a world in drastic need of the news we can bring. So let's get on our feet and go!

I still remember vividly the experience many years ago that ignited my own passion for winning souls. It began when I picked up a hitchhiker on my way home from work. After the bushy-haired young man stuffed his guitar and backpack in my Volkswagen Bug, I introduced myself and learned that his name was Steve. We chatted for a few minutes, and then I offered him a Living Water tract. He took one look at it and sputtered a stream of four-letter words.

"I don't need that. I need a job," he declared.

"Okay, I can get you a job. I'm helping this pastor paint his church and house. I'll let you stay with me and give you free room and board just the same as he's offered me."

Steve agreed, and over the two weeks that it took to finish the job, he opened his heart to Christ. One night in church, I watched as this man, who only days earlier was spewing profanity, stood worshiping the Lord with tears streaming down his face. From that point on, I knew I was "forever ruined for the ordinary." Although I was newly saved myself, I saw that God could use me to win others for Christ. And He has!

God can use *anyone* who is willing to put feet to his or her faith. And the more Christ-like you are, the more effective you will be as His witness. In my interviews with hundreds of Christians about their conversion experience, I have discovered that people are drawn to Christ as much by the character of the messenger of Christ as by the content of their message.

Therefore, in this first section we will examine some characteristics of effective messengers of the Gospel. Our role models are five men, whose lives are documented in the New Testament, who were especially effective in ministry to the lost. Let's find out why.

THE MESSENGER

Characteristics	Biblical Example	Evangelistic Focus	Bottom Line	Relevant Scripture
Servant	Jesus	Heart	The Greatest is servant of all	(Mark 10:43 ◆ 2 Corinthians 4:5)
Simple	Philip	Mouth	Keep it simple	(Acts 8 ◆ 2 Corinthians 11:3)
Supernatural	Peter	Spirit	Not by might, not by power but by God's Spirit	(Zechariah 4:6)
Sacrificial	Stephen	Body	Life comes out of death	(John 12:24 ◆ 2 Corinthians 4:10, 12)
Strategic	Paul	Mind	God's work done God's way brings God's results	(Acts 13-21)

CHAPTER 1

Jesus – Our Role Model of Evangelism

In a book about evangelism, it is fitting that we start with the greatest evangelist who ever lived—our Lord Jesus Christ Himself! Today, many thousands of Christians wear little bracelets with the letters WWJD (What Would Jesus Do?) as a reminder to model their lifestyle after Jesus. As a student of evangelism, I find myself asking another question—how did Jesus do it? He was the holiest person that ever lived and an exact representation of the Father (see Hebrews 1:3), yet He attracted sinners to Himself. His holiness didn't repel the non-believer the way our 21st century "holiness" seems to.

I believe a key difference was His attitude of servanthood. He not only made the ultimate sacrifice of His life for our salvation, He also modeled servanthood in His daily life. Study the Gospels, and you'll see Him constantly laying down His life for other people—teaching them, feeding them, healing them, encouraging them, and ministering to them. He even encouraged us to do good to those who hate us.

Shortly before World War II, Enrico, a Frenchman from an Italian background, bought a lumberyard in Paris. Shortly thereafter, he was converted to Christ. One night while out walking, Enrico discovered two shadowy figures stealing lumber from his property. Enrico shot up a short prayer to heaven and then proceeded to help them load the lumber onto their truck. He went so far as to lead them to other lumber that was even better suited for their purposes.

When he eventually told them he was the owner of the lumberyard, they were afraid he would call the police. Instead, Enrico asked them if he could share a message with them. Within three days, the two men were both converted. One became a pastor and the other a church elder.

After the war started, Enrico realized his lumberyard incident was only a testing ground for servant-evangelism. While being held in a prison camp having been charged with hiding Jews, he was invited into the quarters of the camp commandant on Christmas Day, 1944. The Nazi leader said, "I want you to see the Christmas dinner your wife sent for you before I eat it. She is a good cook! She has sent you a meal every day you have been in prison, and I have enjoyed them all." Enrico, emaciated, pale, and with eyes hollowed from hunger replied, "I hope you enjoy it because I love you." The commandant threw him out thinking he had gone mad.

Two years after the war, Enrico took his wife back to the town in which he was imprisoned only to find his former commandant lived there. Enrico and his wife appeared at his former captor's door with two baskets of his wife's home cooking. Not recognizing the healthy former prisoner, Enrico reminded him of Christmas Day, 1944. He then asked him for the privilege of sharing a meal with the German and his wife. During the meal, Enrico led them both to Christ—a graphic picture of Jesus-style servanthood.[4]

Acts of sacrificial love like these are no doubt what Jesus meant when He said, "Let your light so shine before men, that they may see your good works and glorify your Father in heaven" (Matthew 5:16). Jesus knew that people needed to see the Gospel as well as hear it. He also knew that it helped them to see it when He served them and met them where they were at.

He met the woman caught in adultery with compassion when the religious leaders wanted to stone her (see John 8:1-11). He didn't chastise Nicodemus for coming to Him at night, even though I'll give you two to one odds that Nicodemus' reason for the late night visit was embarrassment to be seen with Jesus. Day or night, Jesus was there to serve.

Recently I boarded an airplane to fly from Hawaii to Los Angeles, and I met an exhausted 19-year-old girl who had spent the night in the Honolulu Airport. As I approached 35A, she looked at me through bloodshot eyes and started to move over to her aisle seat. Knowing as I do (I am an expert on flying!) that window seats are better for sleeping, I offered her my seat. Shortly after the flight was at cruising altitude, I offered her my aisle seat as well so she could lie down. I gave her my pillow and blanket, tucked her in, and proceeded to the back of the plane to do my stretches (which is my custom) and to read my new book on mission's history. After about an hour and a half, I returned to find a rested, happy, and, more importantly, spiritually open young woman. After a couple hours of discussing her need for Jesus, she prayed to receive Him before we landed. The Lord knows if she would have been saved without my friendly overtures, but it certainly didn't hurt to serve her in her area of need.

The Apostle Paul reminded the Corinthians that there must be a "visual" expression of our evangelism when he wrote, "For we do not preach ourselves, but Christ Jesus the Lord, and ourselves your servants for Jesus' sake" (2 Corinthians 4:5). Paul knew that the Corinthians were easily impressed by worldly wisdom but that only the power of humble servanthood would affirm the truth of the Gospel message.

As a non-Christian, I first "saw" the Gospel while working as a dishwasher in a Polish restaurant in California. One of the cooks was a quiet, unassuming guy named Jeff who worked hard and minded his own business. One day the boss's wife, an emotionally challenged micro-manager, berated Jeff for burning potatoes that I knew she had burned herself. When he took the rebuke without defending himself, I later asked him why. He calmly responded that he was a Christian and quoted a phrase about Jesus' command to turn the other cheek when someone strikes you. I didn't quite understand his response at the time, but it left a definite impression on me—one that helped open my heart to Christ.

We must never see our mandate to proclaim the good news of Jesus as simply a verbal message. Jesus-style evangelism gets "down and dirty" and serves people. When Jesus saw the blind beggar, Bartimaeus, He didn't turn away. He approached him and asked, "What do you want Me to do for you?" (Mark 10:51). If we will approach non-Christians with the same attitude, we'll likely see many open their hearts to Christ. Perhaps, the apparent "hardness" we sense from our non-Christian friends or neighbors is simply because they have never seen a Christian take the time to mow their lawn, baby-sit their kids, or invite them for a meal. A large church in southern India sends some of their members to clean up garbage in one of the needy areas near the church and finds the slum dwellers not only appreciative, but also more open to the Gospel. Jesus was a friend of sinners, and we need to follow His example of humble servanthood. Jesus said "...the Son of Man did not come to be served, but to serve, and to give His life a ransom for many" (Matthew 20:28).

STUDY GUIDE

CHAPTER 1

1) Compare Jesus' witnessing style in His various evangelistic encounters. What are the similarities? Distinctives? Principles? In what ways did He serve them?

    a)   Andrew, Peter, Philip, Nathanael (John 1:35-51)

    b)   Nicodemus (John 3:1-17)

    c)   The Samaritan Woman (John 4:1-42)

    d)   The Nobleman (John 4:46-53)

    e)   The Adulterous Woman (John 8:1-11)

    f)   The Blind Man (John 9)

    g)   The Centurion (Matthew 8:5-13)

    h)   The Rich Young Ruler (Matthew 19:16-22 ♦ Mark 10:17-22 ♦ Luke 18:18-23)

    i)   Matthew and those at his house (Matthew 9:9-13)

    j)   Zacchaeus (Luke 19:1-10)

2) Examine the word pictures Jesus used in His teaching on evangelism. How can we apply these to our outreach to the world?

    a)   Fishing (Matthew 4:18-22 ♦ Mark 1:16-18 ♦ Luke 5:1-11)

    b)   Farming (Matthew 13:1-23 ♦ Mark 4:1-20, 26-29 ♦ Luke 8:1-15)

    c)   Being "Born Again" (John 3:3)

    d)   The Lost Sheep and Coin (Luke 15:1-10)

    e)   The Waiting Father (Luke 15:11-32)

f) The Good Shepherd (John 10:1-11)

g) The Bread of Life (John 6)

h) The Water of Life (John 4)

i) The Door to the Sheepfold (John 10:7-9)

3) As we evangelize locally or on the mission field and seek to serve people as Jesus did (feeding, healing, etc.), how can we avoid the malady of producing what has been termed "Rice Christians*"? When Jesus recognized this tendency in people ("...you seek Me, not because you saw the miracles, but because you did eat of the loaves and were filled" (John 6:26)), how did He respond?

* "Rice Christians" is a derogatory term given to people who have responded to the Gospel, not because of conviction of sin and faith in Christ, but because of the services (food, medical care, etc.) that were provided by the Christians reaching out to them.

CHAPTER 2

Keep It Simple
(Profile: Philip)

The only person actually called an evangelist in the New Testament is Philip (see Acts 21:8). In the chapter that gives us most of the information on Philip's life (Acts 8), the word that most characterizes his life is simplicity.

In my studies of church history, I have discovered that simplicity of the message is also a common denominator in the success or failure of the most widely known evangelists. Those who chase various causes or make themselves pseudo-theologians, pop-psychologists, or motivational speakers usually end up dulling the two-edged sword that God has given them to open people's hearts.

The first thing we read about Philip when he began his ministry is that he "went down to a city in Samaria and proclaimed the *Christ...*" (Acts 8:5, NIV, emphasis mine). One of the last things we read about him is that "Philip began with that very passage of Scripture and told him [the Ethiopian eunuch] the good news about *Jesus*" (Acts 8:35, NIV, emphasis mine). Often, in our zeal to reach people for Jesus, we turn to the other disciplines of psychology, sociology, or theology and forget that the essence of evangelism is simply preaching Jesus.

I once saw a cartoon that depicted a supposed "Evangelism Research Laboratory." It pictured people feverishly gathering data on evangelism. Then suddenly, a lab assistant runs in with a read-out proclaiming, "We found it! We found it! The way to evangelize is to tell people about Jesus!" Duh! This satire is truer than we would like to admit. As the world around us changes, we face increasing pressure to adapt our message to be culturally relevant and user-friendly. We are told that this "postmodern" generation is different, and we need new and creative strategies of evangelism to reach them. We must be as creative as we can, but we must not compromise the simple message of Jesus.

The Apostle Paul told the Corinthian believers that, because of their culture, he was tempted to give into the intellectual pressure from the Greek world and use "wise and persuasive words." Instead, he said he would rely on preaching the simple Gospel, which was in "demonstration of the Spirit and of power, that your faith should not be in the wisdom of men but in the power of God" (1 Corinthians 2:4,5).

Francis Schaeffer, one of the most brilliant and influential Christians of the 20th century, was once asked what was the most profound truth he had learned from the Bible. He astounded his interviewer when he replied, "Jesus loves me, this I know, for the Bible tells me so." Though Schaeffer knew all the great truths of Scripture and was an expert in philosophy, he recognized that the Bible's core message was quite simple. In his letter to the Romans, Paul described this simple message as "the power of God to salvation for everyone who believes" (Romans 1:16).

Sadly, the more we learn about God and the Bible, the more we're tempted to complicate both the message and our individual ministries. It is sad but true that, statistically speaking, newly converted Christians make more effective soul winners than those of us who are older in our faith. One of the reasons for this is the inherent simplicity of our new life in Jesus. That's why we'd be wise to heed the sage advice of the late Corrie Ten Boom, who became famous for sheltering Jews in her family's "hiding place" in Holland during World War II. When asked the secret of her ministry, the 85-year-old author summed it up with the acronym K.I.S.S., which stands for Keep It Simple, Stupid! This dear saint, with her delightful Dutch accent and contagious love for Jesus, was reminding the church that if we stray from the simplicity of Christ's message of love and grace, we are in fact stupid!

Even though Philip performed miracles, signs, and wonders to attest to the truth he was preaching, his sole focus was to proclaim the resurrected Christ. He was, in the words of some theologians, "Christ-o-centric" (totally focused on Jesus Christ and Him crucified) (see also 1 Corinthians 2:2). In our day, as various winds of doctrine assail the church, we would do well to follow Philip's example. The landscape of church history is littered with the remains of those who have turned from the simple evangelical Gospel to a social gospel, a liberation gospel, a therapeutic gospel, a prosperity gospel and other diversions. The foundation for all evangelism is Jesus—period.

Another aspect of Philip's simplicity was his single-minded passion for reaching out to the lost (see Acts 8:5-8,12,35,40). An evangelist essentially is a driven person—driven by love for God and love for the world that God created. He is "purpose-driven," the purpose being to proclaim the Gospel. A true evangelist will have lost souls on his mind constantly. He will reach out while on an airplane going to and from meetings, as well as talk about evangelism when he is with other Christians. He will train others to reach the lost. He will share evangelism with his children. He will do everything he can to bring lost people to Jesus. It becomes a magnificent obsession for him or her. I have an evangelist friend named Ray Comfort. Ray will give $1,000 if anyone can catch him without a Gospel tract on his person. Once an aspiring young opportunist grabbed Ray after he got out of a swimming pool—he was hoping to be an instant winner. Ray smiled and pulled a plastic-wrapped tract out of his swim trunks. Ray is always ready. (I wonder if he takes tracts into the shower with him? I have an idea!) Dr. Bill Bright, founder of the world's largest mission organization, Campus Crusade for Christ, warned 4,000 evangelists at Billy Graham's Amsterdam '86 conference, "It is a sad thing that many evangelists do not witness personally and consequently they lose favor with God and man."[5]

Oh, how we need to pray that Philip's passion would multiply in the body of Christ today, that we would have godly evangelists who would be raised up by the Lord, along with the other four ministry gifts in Ephesians 4, "to equip God's people for the work of the ministry"—the ministry of evangelism.

STUDY GUIDE
CHAPTER 2

1) Philip provides us with a model of lifestyle evangelism. Examine his life and see how you can follow his example.

   a) He preached the simple Gospel:
      i) To the masses (Acts 8:5-8)
      ii) Individually (Acts 8:26-38)
      iii) He was consistent (Acts 8:40)
   b) He preached with supernatural power:
      i) He did miracles (Acts 8:6)
      ii) He cast out demons (Acts 8:7)
      iii) He healed the sick (Acts 8:7)
   c) He practiced faithfulness:
      i) He served in practical ways (Acts 6:1-7)
      ii) He was a good "family man" (Acts 21:8-9)
      iii) He knew and used the Scriptures (Acts 8:30-35)
   d) He provided fruit:
      i) Baptized converts (Acts 8:12,38)
      ii) Healing to people sick and in bondage (Acts 8:7)
      iii) "...there was great joy in the city..." (Acts 8:8)

2) Paul warned the Corinthians: "But I fear, lest somehow, as the serpent deceived Eve by his craftiness, so your minds may be corrupted from the simplicity that is in Christ" (2 Corinthians 11:3). He then went on to alert them about counterfeit christs, spirits, and gospels. What would be some other "crafty" ways the enemy could use to seduce us away from Gospel simplicity?

3) Billy Graham has warned fellow preachers over the years about the "3 Gs" of temptation: Gold (money), Girls (sexual immorality), and Glory (pride). How can we safeguard ourselves from the distractions that have pulled many away from simply preaching Christ?

CHAPTER 3

Armed With Supernatural Power

(Profile: Peter)

The information explosion of the last 20 years has greatly helped churches in different parts of the world to communicate more effectively on what God is doing in their neck of the woods. One of the revelations that has come from the data gathered is that much of the church growth in Latin America, Africa, and Asia has come in the churches where people were taught that they served a supernatural, miracle-working God. They simply believed the Bible, and along with preaching the Gospel and teaching the Word, they prayed for the sick, cast out demons, and believed God for miracles. The result: since 1970, more people have come to Christ than in the previous 2,000 years of evangelism.

In my neck of the woods, I was saved during the "Jesus Movement," a time in the late 60s and early 70s where thousands of young people like myself were supernaturally delivered from drugs, eastern religions, and cults by the raw power of Jesus who is "...the same yesterday, today, and forever" (Hebrews 13:8). Pastor Chuck Smith was used by the Lord to father many who were to become leaders in the 21st century church. (Currently, Calvary Chapel has over 1,000 churches worldwide, several of which are some of the largest in America.) When interviewed about the success of those who have been trained through his ministry, he simply smiles and points to God's Word to Zerubbabel: "'Not by might nor by power, but by my Spirit,' says the LORD Almighty" (Zechariah 4:6, NIV).

Jesus spoke of worship being "spirit and truth," the Spirit giving power to the truth. While the Gospel itself is the power of God to bring people to Christ (see Romans 1:16), there is no question that the Lord also uses signs and wonders to affirm the truth of His message.

In this chapter, our role model is the Apostle Peter because his life so clearly illustrates what can happen when an ordinary person moves in the power of the Spirit. At Pentecost, when he and the other apostles were filled with the Holy Spirit, God filled their mouths with heavenly languages that astounded the crowd. Peter proclaimed to the people that this was a sign from God, and he boldly challenged them to believe in Jesus and be cleansed from their sins. That day 3,000 people were saved, and the body of Christ has been growing ever since.

Would the people have believed Peter's message if there had been no miraculous signs accompanying it? Yes, no doubt some would have responded, for the words of the Gospel alone are spiritual dynamite. But when accompanied by a display of God's power, they are like a nuclear blast that melts the hearts of everyone who sees and hears. Paul opened his first letter to the Thessalonians by saying "For our gospel did not come to you in word only, but also in power, and in the Holy Spirit and in much assurance" (1 Thessalonians 1:5).

Supernatural evangelism, however, is not limited to miracles. King David encouraged us that "The steps of a good man are ordered by the LORD" (Psalm 37:23). God can supernaturally direct our steps to be more effective in evangelism. I was in the Albuquerque Airport waiting to board a flight to Honolulu via Denver and San Francisco. Shortly before take-off, the ticket agent announced that due to overbooking, a $400 voucher would be given to anyone willing to wait for a later flight. My hand shot up, and I grabbed my voucher. Amazingly when I got to Denver on a later flight, they had overbooked my flight to San Francisco. I was ready to grab a second voucher when I received an inner "check" in my spirit. I resisted the temptation to go for the money, and I boarded the flight.

A young woman sat next to me who had just been thrown out of her house by her boyfriend. They had both previously attended the Calvary Chapel in their area together, but were backslidden.

A coincidence? Perhaps. However, the fact that I had missed the previous flight, had almost missed her flight, had taught at Calvary Chapels, and had just come from a Calvary Chapel was enough to convince her that it was a "divine appointment." She rededicated her life to Christ on the plane.

On another flight, I was scheduled to go with my wife to a conference when, at the last minute, she threw her back out. Disappointed, I checked in alone for my flight. I was given a complimentary upgrade to First Class because I was flying solo. I just happened to sit next to a young 22-year-old semi-professional baseball player who was ripe and ready to be saved. He gave his life to Jesus before we touched down in San Francisco. Some severe turbulence during the flight "shook him up," which caused him to think about his eternal destiny. A coincidence or supernatural timing? I'll choose to believe the latter since my steps "…are ordered by the LORD" (Psalm 37:23).

There are many instances in the New Testament where people came to Christ as a direct result of the power of God demonstrated by signs, wonders, and miracles. When Peter spoke the word of faith to heal Aeneas, "All those who lived in Lydda and Sharon saw him and turned to the Lord" (see Acts 9:33-35). As word got around Joppa that Peter had raised Tabitha from the dead, "many people believed in the Lord" (see Acts 9:40-42).

Peter is the apostle who let us know that "He is patient with you, not wanting anyone to perish, but everyone to come to repentance" (2 Peter 3:9, NIV). He also told us that God, by "His divine power has given us everything we need for life and godliness…" (2 Peter 1:3, NIV). We need the Bible, our Gospel tracts, anointed preaching, mercy ministries, lifestyle evangelism, love, and sensitivity to reach a lost world. However, we must never think that these things will be sufficient to bring to faith the massive groups of unreached people who are now bound by powers greater than themselves. We need supernatural power accompanying our preaching of the Gospel to bring hardened hearts and blinded minds to Jesus.

The fact that the annual growth rate of churches that believe in and practice the supernatural is twice that of those who do not is no coincidence. People are drawn to Christ when the gifts of the Holy Spirit are functioning in the church and its leaders believe God for supernatural power to heal the sick, cast out demons, and do miracles.

One of the greatest growth spurts of the early church came after God used Peter and John to heal a blind beggar (see Acts 3). As the crowd in Jerusalem was staring in wonder, Peter seized the opportunity to proclaim that it was the resurrection power of Jesus whom they crucified that healed the man. He then challenged them to repent and put their faith in Jesus. Peter's statements disturbed the Pharisees and Sadducees, and they had Peter and John arrested; but 5,000 people believed the message and were saved.

Abdul was a rug salesman in southern India, the son of a Muslim cleric from the north. When confronted with the Gospel by a street drama team, his reply was, "Your religion is stupid. First, Allah does not have a son, and if he did, he surely wouldn't have him killed." The team gave up trying to persuade Abdul, but promised to pray for him. A few nights later, Jesus appeared to him in his room declaring Himself to be the Son of God. Abdul told this writer personally that it was not a dream, but a supernatural vision of Jesus. Today, he and his wife are planting churches among the Muslims in India. Workers in Muslim lands often tell of such supernatural encounters that open sincere Muslims to the grace of God in Jesus.

What About Failure?

Another reason I have chosen Peter to be our profile example of moving in the supernatural in evangelism is his ability to rebound after a failure. Even the most godly leaders, the ones through whom God has most displayed His awesome power, will experience times of frustration and failure. Notables such as John Wesley, D.L. Moody, and Billy Graham were all sorely tempted to give up. We are human, and our flesh sometimes gets in the way of what God wants to do through us. If we don't quit, people will soon see that God is at work in us in spite of our human frailty. As 2 Corinthians 4:7 says, "we have this treasure in earthen vessels, that the excellence of the power may be of God and not of us."

Many times I have felt discouraged and defeated because I have said the wrong thing (or not said anything at all) to someone who desperately needed to hear the Gospel message. There have been times when I have "blown people away" or chickened out in one way or another when faced with an evangelistic opportunity. There have been times when I've talked about heaven when I should have talked about hell and vice versa. Still, in all of these things, God gives us the ability to rebound, and this is because of His supernatural grace that is functioning in our lives. "Though a righteous man fall seven times, he rises again" (Proverbs 24:16, NIV). Peter understood this principle of grace and knew well "the God of the second chance" (see 1 Peter 5:10).

The reason so many Christians can relate to Peter is because of his human frailties. He had blown it big-time. He fell into a stormy sea, and the Lord had to bail him out; he amputated the servant's ear, and the Lord had to heal him; and Peter actually rebuked and denied his Lord! But he was able to turn embarrassing defeats into new opportunities to display the grace and power of God. Perhaps you have been like Peter and have made a mess of things. Perhaps you've been faithless at a time when you sensed God wanted you to believe Him for a miracle. Well, if that is so, don't be discouraged. God will give you other opportunities if you really want to see people won to Christ. You don't have to be a great leader to be used by God in miraculous ways. He is looking for humble, ordinary (and obedient) servants through whom He can display His great power and bring more people to Himself.

STUDY GUIDE
CHAPTER 3

1) Paul warned the Galatians about turning to the energy of the flesh when they had begun in the Spirit (Galatians 3:3). How can we avoid the subtle temptation not to seek for, rest in, and wait for God's power?

2) While recognizing the warnings about religious deception (Matthew 24:5,11,24) and counterfeit miracles and "signs and lying wonders" (2 Thessalonians 2:9), how do we avoid "throwing the baby out with the bath water" and trust God for His power to be released?

3) A point was made about "rebounding" after failure in chapter 3 with Peter as a prime example. How can we avoid the condemnation and despair that is often a result of "blowing it," either in evangelism or our personal life? (See Proverbs 24: 16, "For a righteous man falls seven times, and rises again," NASB.)

DIGGING DEEPER – A

Scriptures dealing with the power of the Word of God to save people.

PASSAGE	POWER OF THE WORD OF GOD	RESULT
1) Romans 1: 16, 10:17; Hebrews 4: 12	God's Word itself contains the power of God.	"...the gospel...is the power of God for the salvation of everyone who believes."

2)	Matthew 5-7	Jesus' Sermon on the Mount.	"When Jesus had ended these sayings…the people were astonished at His teaching, for He taught them as one having authority, and not as the scribes."
3)	Acts 6:1-7	Apostles concentrate on prayer and preaching.	"And the word of God increased; and the number of the disciples multiplied in Jerusalem greatly; and a great company of the priests were obedient to the faith."
4)	Acts 6:10	Stephen preached in the synagogue of the freedmen.	"And they were not able to resist the wisdom and the Spirit by which he spoke."
5)	Acts 8:5-6	Philip preached Christ in Samaria.	"And the people with one accord gave heed to those things which Philip spake…"

6) Acts 9:21   Saul of Tarsus preached Christ in the synagogues.   "…all that heard him were amazed."

7) Acts 10:34-48, 11:14   Peter preached to Cornelius' household.   "While Peter spoke the Holy Spirit fell…he commanded them to be baptized…who shall tell you words where by you and all your house shall be saved."

8) Acts 11:19-21   Unnamed disciples preach at Phoenicia, Cyprus, Antioch to Jews and Greeks.   "And the hand of the Lord was with them and a great number believed and turned to the Lord."

9) Acts 14:1   Paul and Barnabas preach in Iconium.   "…they spoke so effectively that a great number of Jews and also of Greeks believed."

10) Acts 16:12-15   Paul witnessed to Lydia.   "…whose heart the Lord opened that she attended to the things that were spoken by Paul."

See also:

Acts 4:33, 18:24-28, 19:8-10,20, 20:27, 28:24,31 ♦ **Romans** 10: 8-17 ♦ **1 Corinthians** 1:17-18, 2:1-5, 3:1-6, 15:11 ♦ **2 Corinthians** 4:13 ♦ **Ephesians** 6:17 ♦ **Colossians** 1:28 ♦ **1 Thessalonians** 1:5 ♦ **2 Timothy** 4:2,5 ♦ **Titus** 1:3 ♦ **Philemon** 6 ♦ **Hebrews** 2:3-4 ♦ **James** 1:18 ♦ **1 Peter** 1:23-25 ♦ **Revelation** 12:11

DIGGING DEEPER – B

Scriptures dealing with people coming to Christ after experiencing a demonstration of God's supernatural power.

PASSAGE	POWER OF THE HOLY SPIRIT	RESULT
1) John 4:1-42	Jesus reveals knowledge of woman's past.	"Come, see a Man who told me all things that I ever did. Could this be the Christ?"
2) John 4:46-53	Jesus heals nobleman's son.	"…he believed and all his household."
3) John 9	Jesus heals blind man.	"'Lord, I believe.' And he worshipped Him."

4)	Mark 10: 46-52	Jesus heals Bartimaeus.	"…your faith has made you whole, and he followed Jesus in the way."
5)	Acts 8:1-13	Philip heals the sick, casts out demons in Samaria.	"And the people with one accord gave heed to those things which Philip spoke hearing and seeing the miracles which he did."
6)	Acts 9:33-35	Peter informs Aeneas that Jesus had healed him.	"And all they that dwelt at Lydda and Sharon saw him and turned to the Lord."
7)	Acts 9:40-42	Tabitha is raised from the dead.	"And it was known throughout all Joppa: and many believed in the Lord."

8)	Acts 13:6-12	Elymas blinded by Paul.	"Then the deputy, when he saw what was done believed, being astonished at the doctrine of the Lord."
9)	Romans 1:4, 10:9-10	The resurrection of Christ.	"If you believe that God has raised Him from the dead, you will be saved."

See also:

Matthew 10:7-8 ♦ **Mark** 6:7, 16:17-18 ♦ **Luke** 5:17, 9:11,42, 10:
9 ♦ **John** 3:2 ♦ **Acts** 2:43, 5:16, 8:7, 14:3, 15:12, 16:25-26, 19:
11-12 ♦ **Romans** 1:16 ♦ **1 Corinthians** 4:20 ♦ **2 Corinthians** 4:7
♦ **1 Thessalonians** 1:5 ♦ **Hebrews** 2:4

CHAPTER 4

The Seeds of Sacrifice

(Profile: Stephen)

In April of 1999, two troubled teenagers, Eric Harris and Dylan Klebold, walked into Columbine High School in Littleton, Colorado, and began shooting students and teachers in a cold-blooded rampage. In one chilling incident in the library, they confronted a young girl named Cassie Bernall. Pointing a gun in her face, they asked if she believed in God. She said, "Yes," and they responded by shooting her in the head, killing her instantly. Following this unspeakable tragedy, hundreds of teenagers reportedly gave their lives to Christ. They saw something meaningful in the sacrifice of people like Cassie, Rachel Scott, and other Christians who were killed in the school that day—and they reached out to the only Anchor that could hold them in such a terrible time.

In our 21st century pop-style of Western Christianity, the issue of sacrificial suffering or death is foreign to us. We often consider our sufferings abnormal or even demonic, but the Bible gives a different picture. It says that anyone who follows Jesus wholeheartedly will endure sacrifice, suffering, and possibly death. Moreover, the Lord told us to embrace suffering with gladness, for great was our reward in heaven when we would suffer for the Gospel (see Matthew 5:11-12).

I'm not suggesting that if you become a radical for Jesus that you'll be beaten or put to death, but you might be. Jesus is looking for people who will give up their lives to gain His resurrection life. In Mark 8:34-35, He says, "Whoever desires to come after Me, let him deny himself, and take up his cross, and follow Me. For whoever desires to save his life will lose it, but whoever loses his life for My sake and the gospel's will save it."

The essence of ministry is giving up something in order to gain something. We give up our lives so that we may gain Christ and produce good fruit for His kingdom. The Old Testament sacrifices show the sacrifice of animals to gain pardon for sins committed. This priestly system foreshadows for us the reality that all ministry is sacrificed life. If you are truly living for Christ, you are already living a sacrificial life. You are sacrificing time, money, and energy to give yourself to others in ministry. You may have already suffered persecution at home, school, or work for your efforts to minister for Christ. Many seemingly ordinary Christians I know have made huge sacrifices for the kingdom. They do so joyfully because they see that in laying down their lives, they are gaining something of great eternal value.

The history of evangelism shows that many millions have come to Christ as a result not only of the sacrificial lives of Christians but also through their sacrificial deaths. Tertullian, an early church father, once said in response to the Roman authorities who were persecuting the Christians, "the blood of the martyrs is the seed of the church."[6]

That was certainly the case with Stephen, the first martyr of the church. In his life, we have a brief but powerful example of someone who shined his light for Jesus and then gave the ultimate sacrifice so that the Lord would be glorified. We know that as Stephen was stoned to death, they laid his clothes at the feet of a young man named Saul. We can only imagine the deep impact it had on Saul when he witnessed a man about to be killed praying for mercy for his murderers. Soon thereafter, God drew Saul to repentance and faith in Jesus and commissioned him as Paul the apostle, the missionary to the Gentiles. Perhaps it was the vision of Stephen's courage in the face of death that helped give Paul the strength to endure tremendous suffering throughout his long and fruitful ministry (see 2 Corinthians 11). More likely, it was because Paul, like Stephen, kept his eyes fixed on his heavenly goal. He said in Romans 8:18, "I consider that the sufferings of this present time are not worthy to be compared with the glory which shall be revealed in us."

A life sacrificed for Christ always produces good fruit. Jesus said in John 12:24, "I say to you, unless a grain of wheat falls into the earth and dies, it remains alone; but if it dies, it bears much fruit" (NASB). From early church history up until the present day, Christians continue to sacrifice their lives and watch the Lord bring forth much fruit as a result. When the Lord allowed the persecution to come to the early Jerusalem church, it scattered them as fruit-producing seeds because of the martyrdom of Stephen (see Acts 8: 4).

The *World Christian Encyclopedia* says that in the past century, more people have given their lives for Christ than in all of the previous centuries combined. Most are in obscure places in Latin America, Africa, and Asia, and hence get very little "press" in the West. It should also be noted that these are the areas where the most explosive church growth is happening. A coincidence? I think not. God always seems to take the most vicious persecution that Satan inflicts and turns it around for the salvation of more souls.

In early 1999, Australian missionary Graham Staines and his two young sons were burned to death while sleeping in their jeep outside of a Bible camp in India. For over 30 years, Graham and his wife Gladys had dedicated their lives to caring for the lepers in the State of Orissa. Their sacrificial service ran against the prevailing Hindu worldview, which rejects and despises lepers because, according to the doctrines of karma and reincarnation, they deserve to be born that way. The Staines family taught that each leper was precious in God's sight, and their continual show of love toward them eventually provoked a gang of Hindu fanatics to violence.

Soon after the attack, Gladys Staines and her daughter went on national television in India with a public expression of forgiveness toward those who had killed her husband and sons. She also declared their intention to stay in India and to continue their work among the lepers. Her act of Christ-like forgiveness and dedication, in the face of great personal suffering, had a huge impact on the nation's spiritual conscience. Several Hindu Brahmins went on national public television in India and declared that they were ashamed to be associated with what had been done in the name of Hinduism. Many Hindus have since re-examined their beliefs and have come to Christ as a result.

The world would say that people like Graham Staines and Cassie Bernall were fools. However, as another 20th century martyr Jim Elliot once said, "He is no fool who gives up what he cannot keep to gain that which he cannot lose." The wisest thing you can do with your life is to fully surrender it to Jesus Christ.

STUDY GUIDE

CHAPTER 4

1) Elsewhere in this book and in the Bible it is stated that God has promised us an "abundant life" (John 10:10) and "righteousness, peace, and joy in the Holy Spirit" (Romans 14: 17). In our Gospel presentation to people, is there a temptation to offer the "benefits" of the Christian life without emphasizing or even mentioning its demands?

See also:

Matthew 16:24-26 ♦ **Mark** 8:34-38 ♦ **Luke** 14:26-33 ♦ **John** 8:31-32, 12:24-26, 15:8 ♦ **Acts** 9:16

2) In light of our natural human tendency to "love ourselves" ("...For no one ever hated his own flesh," (Ephesians 5:29)), why is it important to study and meditate on the Biblical view of suffering? Consider:

The Suffering of Jesus (Isaiah 50:6, 53:5 ♦ **Mark** 15:34 ♦ **Luke** 22:44 ♦ **Hebrews** 2:10, 5:8, 13:12 ♦ **1 Peter** 1:11,19, 2: 21-24, 3:18, 4:1)

The Persecution of Believers (Matthew 5:11-12 ♦ **Mark** 4: 17 ♦ **Luke** 11:49, 21:12 ♦ **John** 15:20 ♦ **Acts** 4:1-22, 5:17-42, 6:11-15, 7:54-60, 8:1-4, 9:1-3, 11:19, 13:50, 22:4,7, 26: 11 ♦ **Romans** 12:14 ♦ **1 Corinthians** 4:12 ♦ **2 Corinthians** 4:9 ♦ **Galatians** 5:11, 6:12 ♦ **1 Thessalonians** 2:15 ♦ **2 Thessalonians** 1:4 ♦ **2 Timothy** 3:11)

The Suffering of Believers (Matthew 10:22,39, 19:29 ◆ **Acts** 9:16 ◆ **Romans** 8:17,36 ◆ **2 Corinthians** 1:7, 11:23 ◆ **Philippians** 1:29, 3:10 ◆ **Colossians** 1:24 ◆ **1 Thessalonians** 1:6, 2:2, 3:4 ◆ **2 Thessalonians** 1:5 ◆ **2 Timothy** 1:12, 2:12, 3: 11-12, 4:5 ◆ **Hebrews** 11:25 ◆ **James** 5:10 ◆ **1 Peter** 2:20, 3: 14, 4:15, 5:10 ◆ **Revelation** 2:10,13)

The Martyrdom of Believers (Matthew 10:21 ◆ **John** 12:24, 16:2 ◆ **Acts** 7:58, 12:2, 21:13 ◆ **Romans** 8:38 ◆ **1 Corinthians** 13:3 ◆ **Hebrews** 11:37 ◆ **Revelation** 2:13, 6:9, 12:11, 20:4)

Promises for Suffering Believers

Blessedness (Matthew 5:11)

Heavenly rewards (Matthew 5:12)

Heavenly welcome (Acts 7:55)

The glory of God (Romans 8:17-18)

God's comfort (2 Corinthians 1:3-7)

Sharing in Christ's sufferings (Philippians 3:10 ◆ Colossians 1:24 ◆ 1 Peter 4:13)

Joy in suffering (Acts 5:41-42 ◆ Colossians 1:24 ◆ 1 Thessalonians 1:6 ◆ 1 Peter 3:14)

God's retribution (2 Thessalonians 1:6 ◆ Revelation 6:10)

Endurance (Romans 5:3 ◆ James 5:10-11)

Acceptance with God (1 Peter 2:20)

Crown of life (Revelation 2:10)

3) It is evident from the Bible and church history that the quality of the believers' sacrificial lives (and in many cases their deaths) contributed immensely to the reception of the message they preached. How can we (without resorting to legalism) follow their example and live a God-centered life as opposed to a self-centered life?

CHAPTER 5

Spirit-Led Strategies

(Profile: Paul)

If we are not careful in our efforts to reach the lost, we can polarize our thinking regarding evangelism. There are some crying out for more detailed strategic planning, research, and careful evaluation of our efforts to be better stewards of God's resources. Others say no, away with such humanistic efforts at accomplishing divine goals. All we need is the Holy Spirit.

I can think of no greater example of a balance between the two than the Apostle Paul. In fact, I don't see in Paul's evangelism conflicting poles, but a beautiful strategy that was in fact planned by the Holy Spirit.

In the opening verses of Acts chapter 17, we find the Apostle Paul establishing a new church in the Macedonian city of Thessalonica. Because of his efforts, a thriving base for the evangelization of Macedonia is founded, to which he would later address the letters of First and Second Thessalonians. Paul opens his first letter by commending the Thessalonian believers for their great evangelistic zeal, faith, hope, and love in Christ. He goes on to say that because their evangelizing had been so effective throughout the entire region, on a later visit his team had "no need to say anything" (1 Thessalonians 1:8, NASB). Now that is effective.

Paul's success in church planting at Thessalonica highlights some important principles of evangelistic strategy. If we study the 17th chapter of Acts along with the Thessalonian epistles, we find it only took Paul three weeks to plant that church. Under the guidance of the Holy Spirit, the strategies gleaned here can be used in other situations to promote effective evangelism with long-lasting results. We must be careful, however, not to copy Paul's example without first having God's leading. The Holy Spirit is the one who will show us how to apply these principles in our own particular situations. "Unless the Lord builds the house, they labor in vain who build it" (Psalm 127:1).

Identification

Paul made a point of identifying with the people he was trying to reach (see Acts 17:1-2). He allowed his unbelieving audience to shape what he would say and how he would say it. Acts chapter 17 records Paul ministering in four different locations—Thessalonica, Berea, Athens, and on Athens' Mars' Hill.

In the first three instances, the apostle preached in synagogues. In some cases, the Scriptures indicate that he opened to Isaiah or the Psalms in order to show that Jesus Christ was the fulfillment of all that was foretold in the Jewish Scriptures. He did not preach to the philosophers of Mars' Hill from the Jewish scriptures, though, as these writings were inauthoritative to pagan philosophers. Instead, Paul found a point of interest from which he could communicate with them. Pointing to the altar of the unknown god—an open door through which he could share the same truth as he had in the synagogue—he was able to identify with the group.

Paul realized that preaching from Jewish Scriptures in the Thessalonian synagogue presented the truth in a way the Jews could understand. Likewise, speaking of the Creator God and quoting from their own Greek poets allowed Paul to identify with the philosophers on Mars' Hill and help them grasp what he was saying. That's communicating!

Jesus Christ is our supreme example of identification. He became one of us in order that He might reach us. In the same way, Paul explained that he had become "all things to all men, that I may by all means save some" (1 Corinthians 9:22).

Finding correct balance between identification with and separation from the world is not always easy. Just how far we should go is between each individual and the Lord, and we need to look continually to Him for that balance. There are instances, however, when it is necessary to step outside cultural norms.

Hudson Taylor, a young man with a burden for China, took the bold step of leaving England to live among the Chinese. Finding himself largely ineffective on sharing with the Chinese, Taylor realized the need for greater identification with the people he wanted to reach. Therefore, he began to eat Chinese food, learned the Chinese language, and grew his hair until it was long enough to braid.

Although Taylor was frowned upon by many of his contemporary missionaries and widely misunderstood at home, his results were astounding. Eventually he founded one of the most successful cross—cultural missionary movements in the history of the church—the China Inland Mission Society—which still thrives today as the Overseas Missionary Fellowship.

In 1962, Don and Carol Richardson moved to Irian Jaya as missionaries to the cannibalistic, stone-aged Sawi people. Here they found a people hardened to the Gospel, among whom treachery was considered the highest virtue. When Don and Carol tried to explain the death and resurrection of Christ to the Sawi, they saw Judas as the hero of the story. His kiss of betrayal delighted them as the ultimate act of virtue.

Seeking God for an answer to their dilemma, the Richardsons witnessed a cultural ritual that enabled them to unlock the true meaning of the Gospel to the Sawi. They observed that when the Sawis made peace with a certain enemy tribe, they would exchange babies as a covenant of peace. If either of the children died, the covenant would be broken, and war would resume. But as long as the children lived, there would be peace between the tribes. Anyone who would kill the "peace child" would himself be killed. Don and Carol explained to the Sawi that Jesus was God's Peace Child whom He had sent to bring reconciliation between Himself and the world. They further pointed out that God was able to use the death of His Peace Child as the means of their forgiveness.

This new perspective on the Gospel eventually resulted in many of the tribe accepting the peace of Christ as they were reconciled to God. These two sensitive missionaries were able to see a major breakthrough of the Gospel among the Sawi because they had identified with them and their culture.

Building Bridges, Crossing Cultures

Paul found much common ground with those he was seeking to evangelize. A study of his missionary journeys shows a definite and carefully planned strategy in the visits he made to various cities of the ancient world. It was no coincidence that Athens was the intellectual center of the Empire: Rome was the capital; Philippi was the chief Roman colony in Macedonia; Ephesus was home to the largest temple to a false goddess; and Corinth was the Empire's "sin city." The Holy Spirit gave him strategies on every stop in his journeys. He would go to a city, find the local synagogue, and seek to preach the Gospel there. Acts 17:2 tells us this was "his custom." The synagogues contained three groups of people: Jews (natural children of Israel); Jewish proselytes (Gentiles who had converted to Judaism via circumcision); and God-fearers (Gentiles who believed in and feared God but who stopped short of becoming proselytes).

Often rejected and persecuted by the Jewish sector, Paul would form the nucleus of his new church from the God-fearing Gentiles, who already believed in the God of the Old Testament and needed only to be instructed in the Gospel message. They were "ripe," and Paul took advantage of their scriptural heritage to reap a rich harvest of souls in the places he visited.

When Jesus spoke of the harvest field, He spoke of entering into another man's labors (see John 4:38). Paul understood what this meant and, as it were, harvested where the Jews had already planted the seed.

Comparing the apostle's results in Thessalonica—where there *was a heritage factor* and where "many of them therefore believed, along with a number of prominent Greek women and men" (Acts 17:12, NASB)—and Mars' Hill—where there *was no heritage factor* and only a few believed (Acts 17:35)—is very enlightening. Paul went to the religious people first, in much the same way Jesus went to the Jews (see Matthew 15:24). The Gospel was to go to the Jews first, and the Gentiles would be grafted in at a later date (see Romans 1:16 and Romans 11).

In many nations today where significant church growth is occurring, much of the groundwork had already been done by earlier Christian workers who gave the people a heritage factor and rendered them receptive to the Gospel. In Latin America, for example, the Catholic missionaries laid the groundwork that has resulted in rapid growth of the churches in Brazil, Guatemala, Argentina, and other countries of the region. The same is true of the Protestant missionaries who pioneered the way for the staggering growth of the churches in South Korea, Indonesia, South Africa, and even North America.

I met John Pipolo one day while street witnessing, and my wife and I soon became good friends with him and his brother, Anthony. They were in a sense true 20th century "God-fearers" from a strong Italian Catholic background. We began visiting them from time to time to share the Gospel, but eventually we lost contact with each other. Other Christians, though, shared the love of Jesus with them through both personal testimony and literature. John and Anthony were encouraged to follow Jesus, and eventually they did along with John's wife, mother, sister, and older brother. Today, some of the most committed Christians I know are within the Pipolo family. Their strong Catholic heritage provided a wonderful foundation on which to build.

A common mistake made by many in their zeal to "contend earnestly for the faith" (Jude 3) is to disregard the heritage factor. In our desire to "set people straight" about their beliefs, we often end up alienating them from us. When we attack a Roman Catholic over their belief in the mass, the rosary, or the Virgin Mary, we destroy the foundation God has given us to build on in their life. The foundation may be faulty, but it is nonetheless an excellent starting point to lead them to the truth. We can't allow ourselves to be sidetracked from the central issue—their relationship with Jesus Christ.

I envision our witnessing as building a bridge—a relationship bridge—which will allow us to walk over the "communication gap" into the non-Christian's world and heart with the truth. The gap can be linguistic, racial, cultural, or religious, but it hinders us from communicating God's truth.

Often in attacking a person's beliefs, in effect we blow up the bridge God wants us to build! We should take advantage of the heritage factor and build upon it, realizing it can be a great help in conveying the truth.

Building bridges across cultural barriers is not easy. Often those of us from the West view life in easily divided compartments. Not so in many non-Western nations. Things like religion, culture, language, family, and tradition are woven together and overlap in almost every decision that is made, including the decision of whether or not to follow Jesus. To use a simple illustration, we see life like a TV dinner with the meat, potatoes, vegetables, and desert nicely separated. They see life as a stew!

Another point to keep in mind is that when we cut down someone else's beliefs (for instance, an Italian, Mexican, or Filipino), they don't see it as simply a disagreement over religion, but an attack on who they are! They are culturally "Catholic" and see themselves *born* that way. A Tibetan is *born* a Buddhist. An Indian is *born* a Hindu, etc. Eventually, of course, there will come a conflict when the truth is made clear, but I believe a key in witnessing is lifting up Jesus Christ and watching Him draw people to Himself.

In discussing the heritage factor, I am not suggesting that we attempt to reach only those with "suitable" backgrounds. There are millions of people not receptive to the Gospel who have no heritage factor, and we need workers to prepare the way for them to receive the message of salvation. If, however, we are in an area that has a Christian heritage, it will be to our distinct advantage to build upon it as we share the Gospel.

Consistency

Paul was consistent in his evangelism, "according to his custom" (Acts 17:2). He understood that if you sow sparingly, you will also reap sparingly, and his evangelism reflected this principle (see 2 Corinthians 9:6).

A farmer doesn't just sow a few seeds here and there and expect to gather in a great harvest. Instead, he prepares the ground carefully and plants a lot of seeds. Likewise, no commercial fisherman will fish only when he *feels* like it but will continually let down his nets and reposition his boat until he has an adequate catch. From this we can learn an important lesson. We must be consistent not only in planting the seed of the Gospel in people's hearts but also in watering that seed. Often we give up on a person we've witnessed to because there was no immediate response. What's really needed is to build a relationship with the person. Then, over time, we are more likely to see them come to the Lord.

The bottom line on Paul's strategy was made clear when he told the Corinthians he "became all things to all men, that by all means I might save some" (see 1 Corinthians 9:22). He argued with the Jerusalem Council in Acts 15 that the Gentiles did not have to be circumcised to become Christian, yet in the very next chapter he urged his young Gentile convert, Timothy, to be circumcised! Why? "...because of the Jews who lived in the area" (Acts 16:3, NIV). He was building a bridge to the Jews.

Back to Acts 17, as noted earlier, Paul not only used the altar to the unknown god as an interest door but quoted the Greek Stoic and Epicurean poets to make his point. He was a bridge-builder. That was his strategy.

STUDY GUIDE

CHAPTER 5

1) The point of chapter 5 is the Biblical balance of supernatural guidance and Spirit-led, "sanctified common sense" in the evangelistic strategy of the early church. Consider the following random survey of the Holy Spirit's work in guiding the early Christians in evangelism.

Strategy and Guidance in the Book of Acts

Supernatural	Supernaturally Natural
Acts 2:1-4 – Spirit poured out at Pentecost.	**Acts 2:44-45** – Distribution of material goods.
Acts 5:19 – Angelic deliverance.	**Acts 5:34-40** – Human deliverance.
Acts 6:8 – Stephen's miracle ministry.	**Acts 6:1-7** – Seven Hellenist leaders appointed over Hellenist food distribution.
Acts 8:4-8 – Philip's miracle ministry.	**Acts 8:1-4** – Believers flee persecution.
Acts 9:1-9 – Saul supernaturally blinded, struck down and audibly spoken to by Jesus.	**Acts 9:23-25** – Saul delivered in a basket with a little help from his friends.
Acts 11:28 – Agabus gives supernatural prophecy about famine.	**Acts 11:29** – The disciples take an offering.

Acts 13:1-4 – The Holy Spirit spoke to the Antioch leaders to send out Barnabas and Saul.

Acts 13:4 – Their first stop was Cyprus, Barnabas was from Cyprus (Acts 4:36). A coincidence?

Acts 15:1-11 – Paul, Barnabas, and Peter declare the supernatural work of God among the Gentiles.

Acts 15:13-31 – James, apostles, and elders give four common sense prohibitions to Gentile converts as not to offend the Jews.

Acts 16:6-10 – The Holy Spirit speaks: don't go to Asia or Bithynia. The Holy Spirit gives Paul a vision calling him to Macedonia.

Acts 16:1-3 – Paul has Timothy circumcised as not to offend the Jews.

Acts 16:12 – Paul goes to Philippi because of the vision.

Acts 16:12 – Philippi is "the chief city of that part of Macedonia."

Acts 16:26 – Paul and Silas supernaturally delivered by an earthquake.

Acts 23:12-17 – Paul's nephew overhears about plot to kill Paul, informs him who, then tells centurion who provides Roman protection for Paul.

Acts 17 – Paul preaches the Gospel with great power in Thessalonica, Berea, and Athens.

Acts 17 – Thessalonica, Berea, and Athens all have synagogues (1,10,17). Athens was the intellectual capital of the empire.

Acts 18:9-10 – God speaks to Paul in a vision regarding Corinth.

Acts 18:1-4 – Paul stays in Aquila and Priscilla's house "for by their occupation they were tent-makers" – so was Paul. Corinth was a main commercial center.

Acts 19 – God's power is demonstrated in Ephesus in "special miracles" (11) and "mighty" church growth (20).

Acts 19 – Ephesus was a commercial center as well as home of the largest, most influential pagan temple in the world (27).

Acts 20 – Paul was persuaded the Holy Spirit was leading him to Jerusalem (16,22,21:13).

Acts 21 – Jerusalem was the Holy city, birthplace of Christianity, and home to the Apostles.

Acts 22-30 – Paul ended up in Rome, the capital of the empire through a series of supernatural (i.e. word of knowledge on the ship [27:22-24] and healing from a deadly snake bite [28:3-6]), and supernaturally natural (he spoke Greek and Hebrew [21:37,40] and was a Roman citizen [21:39]) influences.

Illustrated in the above survey is that the Holy Spirit sovereignly led the evangelistic strategy of the early Christians in the way He deemed appropriate. Our danger is to put the Holy Spirit "in a box" and not continually seek His guidance in every aspect of our strategy, whether obviously supernatural or naturally supernatural.

2) Chapter 5 speaks of one of Paul's main evangelistic strategies—identifying with the people he was trying to reach. Compare the balance in the Scriptures between identification with the world and separation from the world.

Identification	Separation
1 Corinthians 9:20-23	Romans 12:1-2
Matthew 11:19	1 John 2:15-17
Luke 7:34	James 4:4
Acts 16:1-3	2 Corinthians 6:17

3) In Acts 17, Paul is involved in five separate evangelistic situations—Thessalonian synagogue, Berean synagogue, Athens' synagogue, Athens' marketplace, and Athens' "Areopagus." Compare his different strategies and apply them to the 21st century.

SECTION II

The Message of the Good News

When the *H.M.S. Titanic* slammed into an iceberg and began sinking, she sent out an SOS message, hoping a nearby ship would come to her rescue. The steamship *California* was a scant ten miles away and had sufficient room for all the *Titanic's* passengers and crew. She could even see the *Titanic's* sidelights in the distance. However, there was one fatal problem: the radio operator on the *California* had turned off the ship's radio. The desperate message that could have saved hundreds of lives was never received.

Perhaps the only thing more tragic than a life-saving message being lost is for it to come through confused or untruthful. From the moment Jesus commissioned the church to proclaim His good news in all the world, there have been unceasing efforts to pervert or challenge the truth of His message. From the sinister heresies of the Dark Ages to the cults and "isms" of today, the life-giving message of the Gospel has been twisted in a thousand different ways. Today, the electronic and print media are churning out more confusing and conflicting messages about Jesus than in all of the previous centuries combined. Jesus Himself predicted that toward the last days there would be widespread religious deception (see Matthew 24:5,11,24). Paul also warned the Corinthians about preaching another Jesus, another gospel, and another spirit (see 2 Corinthians 11:4). For this reason, it is more vital than ever that Christians understand and be able to explain the core message of the Gospel.

In this section, we will examine that message. We start by seeking to establish the truth of the Gospel while learning how to answer the arguments of those who believe there is no truth. We then focus on the core message: faith in Jesus, repentance, grace, baptism, and eternal life. These may seem like old themes to many of us, but if we don't present them clearly, there can be eternal consequences. This is the only message by which humankind may be saved.

THE MESSAGE

Contents	Biblical Principle	Evangelistic Focus	Bottom Line	Relevant Scripture
Truth	The truth sets free	Absolute truth	What we believe	(John 8:32)
Repentance	Repent or perish	Sin	What we are saved from	(Luke 13:5 ◆ Matthew 1:21)
Uniqueness	No other name	Salvation	Who saves us	(John 14:6 ◆ Acts 4: 12)
Trust	Without faith we cannot please God	Faith	What message saves us	(I Corinthians 15:1-4 ◆ Hebrews 11:6)
Heaven	It's the Gospel of the kingdom	Eternity	Where we will spend eternity	(John 3:16 ◆ I John 5: 13)

CHAPTER 6
True Truth

Pontius Pilate, the Roman governor, was presiding over the trial of Jesus when he heard Him declare, "I have come to bear witness to the truth. Everyone who is of the truth hears My voice" (see John 18:37). Pilate responded bluntly, "What is truth?" He then turned and walked away. Perhaps if he had hung around for a few minutes, He who is truth incarnate would have answered his question.

The Ultimate Question

Pilate's question is at the heart of all questions about religion. Every philosophy seeks to answer the questions, "What is truth? Is there such a thing? Is it relative? Is it absolute? Does it really matter?"

The answer is yes, there is an ultimate truth, and yes, it does matter whether you believe it. Jesus made that clear when He said, "I am the way, the truth, and the life. No one comes to the Father except through Me" (John 14:6).

Yet, we must be willing to engage in open discussion with those who disagree. When I am sharing with someone from another religion, I acknowledge to them that my belief, as well as theirs, is a matter of faith for the present and hope for the future, neither of which can be "proved" in the empirical sense. However, as I start to contrast the differences between our two beliefs, the truth becomes more evident. The great British preacher, C.H. Spurgeon, once said that he didn't like to argue about religion, but instead was in favor of laying down his straight rod next to their crooked one and letting them decide which one to pick up! Believing as I do that Jesus is the truth, I know the truth of Christianity will prevail.

Therefore, when talking with a Hindu or New Ager, for example, I start by agreeing about our common quest for truth. Then I move on to the differences in our beliefs. Hindus believe they go through a series of reincarnations. Therefore, I would say something along this line: "I believe we are born once, die once, and face one judgment based on what we have done with Jesus Christ and His Gospel. As a result of that choice, we will spend eternity in one of two places—heaven or hell. As a Hindu, you believe that we have lived many lifetimes and died many times. Based on your religious performance during those lifetimes, you believe we will either progress or digress on the cycle of birth and rebirth."

"Now we obviously have diametrically opposed viewpoints on what happens to us when we die and what we do to determine our destiny. Since neither of us has actually 'been there and done that,' we can both agree absolutely on three things. Either: (1) I am right and you are wrong; (2) you are right and I am wrong; or (3) we are both wrong. We cannot both be right." I then go on to proclaim the simple Gospel in the clearest possible way, praying that he or she will "pick up the straight rod."

When an agnostic or skeptic challenges me on the absoluteness of truth, I ask questions that show they base numerous decisions on their belief that some things are absolutely true and others are not. For example, I ask what they would do if they handed a bank teller a check for $300 and were given $30 in return. Would they shrug their shoulders and accept that the only difference between $300 and $30 is a decimal point? Or would they insist on being given the *true* amount? I dare say they would demand the other $270!

I ask if they stop at red lights and why. I ask if they jump off the roofs of tall buildings and why not. And I ask what predetermined conclusions they have about a pilot's abilities when they step on an airplane. After demonstrating how often people make decisions based on their perceptions of what is true, I then point out that this is also true of spiritual things. If they insist that truth is relative to the individual, I ask if they are *absolutely* sure!

Truth on Trial

So how does a person arrive at an understanding of truth, or in our case, the ultimate truth? The heretical Gnostics in Bible times said that truth came by an inner "knowledge" given to a select few. Modern existentialist philosophers say truth is arrived at by practical experience. Empiricists say that truth is obtained by observation and experiment. Rationalists believe truth is discovered by reason. Mystics say it comes through religious experience, while traditionalists say it comes through culture and ritual (we've always done it this way, therefore it must be true). The Deists and Determinists say it has all been set in motion beforehand, and if you're not one of the chosen, you could not discover truth if you wanted to!

These descriptions are a bit over-generalized, but they do give an overview of various forms of epistemology (methods of arriving at knowledge or truth). By contrast, we receive truth, and therefore freedom, through faith in Jesus Christ (see John 8:31-32). He sent His Holy Spirit (also known as the Spirit of truth) for the specific purpose of guiding us into all truth. So, does this mean that we need not attempt to prove the Gospel? Not at all. Some of our strongest ammunition for affirming the life-changing truth of the Gospel is both our defense of it and our giving evidence for it. Consider the following courtroom scenario:

I am teaching an evangelism class which you and 50 other students have attended faithfully every weeknight from 7 to 9 p.m. One night, two police officers come in and arrest you on suspicion of murder. Shocked and bewildered, you are taken away to the station house. I become your attorney and start mounting a defense. The strongest evidence against you is the alleged murder weapon, a baseball bat that has some of the victim's blood and hair imbedded on the end and your fingerprints on the handle. As I examine the evidence, I try to determine the time of the murder. The coroner has determined the blow to the victim's head occurred approximately 8 p.m. on Monday night. I then line up my 50 witnesses who testify that you were in my class at that time on Monday night. I also produce witnesses who saw you with the bat in your hand at the Sunday afternoon church picnic playing softball. This explains your prints on the handle. After considering this evidence, the jury acquits you unanimously.

Have I <u>proved</u> absolutely that you are innocent? No. The only way I could do that would be to show a videotape replay of the actual murder. However, I have presented evidence to convince the jury "beyond a reasonable doubt" that you are not guilty.

This is how we bear witness to the truth of the Gospel. We are witnesses who testify to what we have seen, heard, and experienced (see Acts 4:20). The non-Christian is the jury who must decide if the evidence you are presenting is sufficient for them to render a verdict for Christ. "Now faith is the substance of things hoped for, the evidence of things not seen" (Hebrews 11:1, KJV). We cannot make them believe or absolutely prove the truth of the Gospel. However, we can present overwhelming evidence upon which they can base their faith.

When people are open to the Gospel, I keep dishing out more and more truth to them. Just hearing the truth does not convert a person, but the more we give them, the more <u>capacity</u> they have to believe. In time, the Holy Spirit will lift the blinders off their eyes so they can respond in faith. Jesus said, "You shall know the truth, and the truth shall make you free" (John 8:32).

STUDY GUIDE
CHAPTER 6

1) Recent surveys have demonstrated that the 21st century "postmodern" culture largely rejects the concept of absolute truth. Since God's truth does not change, consider ways to communicate God's truth to postmodernists.

2) Jesus spoke of the power of truth to set people free if they continue in His Word (John 8:31-32). Consider and contrast the following benefits to those who obey the truth and consequences for those who do not. See how you can use these insights in your evangelism.

Benefits of Walking in Truth

a) Truth helps us worship God in spirit because He is the Spirit of truth (John 4:23-24, 14:17, 15:26, 16:13).

b) Truth helps us discern manifestations of the Spirit (1 Corinthians 12:7) by manifestations of the truth (2 Corinthians 4:2).

c) Truth sanctifies us (John 17:17 ♦ 2 Thessalonians 2:13).

d) Truth helps expose lies (Romans 1:18, 25 ♦ 1 John 2:4, 21, 27).

e) Truth is a part of our spiritual armor (Ephesians 6:14) and is a spiritual weapon (Ephesians 6:17 ♦ Luke 4:1-13).

f) Truth about Jesus saves us (2 Thessalonians 2:13 ♦ 1 Timothy 2:4).

g) Truth "purifies our souls" (1 Peter 1:22).

h) Truth "establishes" us (2 Peter 1:12).

i) Truth helps us know God's grace (Colossians 1:6).

j)　Truth motivates us to good works (1 John 3:17-18).

On The Other Hand, Truth Can Be:

a)　**Neglected**—resulting in "controversy with God" (Hosea 4:1).

b)　**Suppressed**—resulting in God's wrath (Romans 1:18).

c)　**Disobeyed**—resulting in "tribulation and anguish" (Romans 2:8, 9).

d)　**Disbelieved**—resulting in damnation (2 Thessalonians 2:12).

e)　**Destitute**—resulting in a "corrupt mind" (1 Timothy 6:5).

f)　**Resisted**—resulting in reprobation and corruption (2 Timothy 3:8).

g)　**Turned away from**—resulting in distraction and believing "myths" (1 Timothy 4:4 ♦ Titus 1:14).

h)　**Wandered from**—resulting in death (James 5:19).

i)　**Evil spoken of**—resulting in destruction (2 Peter 2:2).

j)　**Absent from us**—resulting in self-deception (1 John 1:8).

3)　It has been said by some: "We don't have to defend the truth because the truth defends itself." How are we to respond to this statement in light of the following passages?

a)　**Psalm 19**—The creation speaks of God's existence.

b)　**Romans 1:20**—God's created order renders men "without excuse."

c)　**Romans 10:17-18**—God's word is "announced" by His creation.

d)　**Acts 7**—Stephen's defense before the Sanhedrin.

e) **Acts 14:15-18**—Paul and Barnabas appeal to God's creation to open the door to the Gospel.

f) **Acts 17:22-31**—Paul appeals to God's creation, the "Unknown God" altar, and both the Stoic and Epicurean philosophers to open the door for the Gospel.

g) **Acts 22**—Paul's defense in Jerusalem.

h) **Philippians 1:7-17**—Paul describes his "ministry of defense" for the Gospel.

i) **1 Peter 3:15**—Peter tells us to "be ready to answer" everyone who asks us about our hope.

j) **Jude 3**—Jude exhorts us to "earnestly contend for the faith."

CHAPTER 7
The First Word of the Gospel

I once heard an anecdote about an evangelist who was obsessed with counting "scalps"—the number of those who had been saved at his crusades. With little regard for integrity or follow-up, he had a tendency to report everything that moved in his meetings as a conversion to Christ. Hence, his reporting was more than slightly 'evang*elastic*.' He died, went to heaven, and stood before the Lord. When the books were opened, he was anxious to get his heavenly rewards for his harvested fruit. Expecting to see thousands of souls lining the streets of gold, he was shocked to see three people. He was bewildered as the Lord explained that those three were saved *in spite* of the message he preached!

Our evangelist friend didn't consciously water down the Gospel message. Rather, in his efforts to be "user-friendly" or culturally appropriate in his presentations, he neglected to emphasize the first word of the Gospel. That word is repentance, and it's one thing we must never compromise on in our message. God has initiated a covenant with us in which he offers forgiveness of sins and eternal life through the blood of Jesus. Our part in this covenant is to accept and respond to His conditions for salvation. While God's love for us is unconditional (see John 3: 16), His salvation is certainly conditional. His two conditions are repentance and faith.

The first commandment that ever fell from the lips of Jesus Christ was to repent. As He began His public ministry as recorded in Mark 1:14-15, He declared, "The time is fulfilled, and the kingdom of God is at hand. Repent, and believe in the gospel." He was making it clear that the primary reason for His coming was to preach repentance. He said, "I have not come to call the righteous, but sinners, to repentance" (Luke 5:32). He also declared that if we would not repent, we would perish (see Luke 13:5). His last commandment was similar to the first that "repentance and forgiveness of sins will be preached in his name to all nations..." (Luke 24:47, NIV).

True repentance is the outworking of true faith. In the mind of Jesus, they are not mutually exclusive actions. He linked them together when He said that the Ninevites "repented at the preaching of Jonah" (see Luke 11:32). The account in the Book of Jonah, however, records that they "believed God" and makes no specific mention of repentance (see Jonah 3:5). By inference, we conclude that repentance and faith are inseparably linked. The call to faith and the call to repentance are one and the same. The great evangelist, John Wesley, actually warned of false conversions where people would give "mental assent" to certain truths of the Gospel without a heart-belief that resulted in a changed life. He understood that Biblical salvation meant a dual turning away *from* sin and idolatry (repentance) *to* Jesus Christ (faith). Paul, in his farewell to his friends at Miletus, said he had declared, "To both Jews and Greeks that they must turn to God in repentance and have faith in our Lord Jesus" (Acts 20:21, NIV).

Whenever I am seeking to explain to someone what they need to do to get right with God, I use this simple illustration: "Let's say you're walking down the street heading north, and across the street you notice that Jesus is heading south. He calls out your name, points to you with His nail-scarred hands, and beckons you to follow Him. At this point, you must make a decision for or against Christ. If you really believe that the man across the street is Jesus, the Son of God and Savior of the world, your reasonable response will be to turn from going your own way and follow Jesus. From that point on, you go wherever He leads." So now the question: can half of you follow the Lord while the other half follows the world? Not if you've repented and believed. The arguments about whether you can be lost once you're saved or whether you can accept Jesus as Savior and not embrace Him as Lord become unnecessary in the light of true repentance.

Can you imagine Jesus going up to His disciples and asking them to accept Him as their personal Savior and not require them to follow Him as Lord? No way! The Gospel is God-centered, not man-centered. It revolves around the glory of God, not the happiness of man. I get deeply concerned when Jesus is presented simply as a personal Savior who will meet people's needs. He is not some sugar daddy in the sky, a washing powder that washes whiter, or a trip to end all trips. He is the Lord of the universe, and He demands our total surrender.

I have heard the Gospel presented in such a way that Jesus seems like a divine pizza pie that can be sliced and selected according to our preferences! There is the Savior slice for those who don't want to go to hell; the Healer slice for those who don't want to be sick; a Provider slice for those who don't want to be poor; and a Lover slice for those who don't want to be lonely. Then there are the slices of Master and King, which are often presented as optional extras. Salvation is offered on the installment plan. The idea of "making Jesus Lord" at some later time in our spiritual development would have been ludicrous to the early disciples. They knew that you don't <u>make</u> Jesus Lord; He <u>is</u> Lord. That this point even needs comment shows how far we have fallen from Jesus' teachings on repentance.

Not long ago, I was preaching at a church, and I gave an invitation at the end of the message for those who wanted to receive Christ. One of those responding was a rather rough-looking guy in his early 30s. As I put my hand on his shoulder to ask how I could pray for him, he collapsed to the floor sobbing. When I went to comfort him, I sensed the Holy Spirit saying, "Don't comfort him. He needs to feel the conviction of sins committed." He then confessed to me his sins one-by-one. He recounted how he had hurt his family, friends, and God with his selfish lifestyle. After he felt sufficiently guilty, I led him to Christ.

I believe that one reason we have so many "backsliders" in the church today is that they have never slid forward enough in the first place! Never feeling the weight of sins committed, they never feel the joy of sins forgiven. True repentance makes the "bad news" of sin and judgment sufficiently bad so the "good news" of forgiveness can be appreciated.

Accessing God's Amazing Grace

One blessing of repentance is that it opens our eyes to the wonder of God's grace. We once were blind to the consequences of our sin, but as we experience conviction leading to repentance, a light begins to dawn. In time, we see the terrible price God paid for our salvation. By His righteous standards, we were deserving of the death penalty, but instead Jesus took that penalty for us. He gave us the very thing we didn't deserve—forgiveness and eternal fellowship with God. That's the wonder of His amazing grace.

Dietrich Bonhoeffer, the German theologian who was martyred during the Holocaust, once described the value that God places on His grace: "Such grace is costly because it costs a man his life, and it is grace because it gives him the only true life. It is costly because it condemns sin and grace because it justifies the sinner. Above all, it is costly because it cost God the life of His Son. 'You were bought with a price,' and what has cost God so much cannot be cheap for us."[7]

Somehow, we have taken what Bonhoeffer called the cost of discipleship and made it an optional extra for those Christians who want to get serious with Jesus. I find it interesting that the word *disciple* is mentioned 269 times in the New Testament, while the word Christian is mentioned only 3 times. Jesus said make disciples, not just decisions, and without repentance, this is impossible.

In our witnessing, we must never compromise this message of repentance for the sake of an increased number of converts. Repentance is not only necessary for forgiveness of sins, but for entrance into the kingdom of God (see Mark 1:14-15) and reaching maturity in Christ (see Hebrews 6:1). It produces fruit that shows we've been truly changed by God.

Chuck Colson tells the story of his friend Jack Eckerd (owner of the Eckerd Drug Store chain). Jack had heard about Chuck's Prison Fellowship ministry and supported his efforts for prison reform. Though Jack was not a committed Christian, he would travel with Chuck on speaking tours and listen patiently as Chuck witnessed to him about the Gospel. One day Jack gave Chuck a call and said that he finally had come to believe that Jesus died on the cross and rose from the dead for his sins. Colson exclaimed, "Then you are born-again!" Even though Eckerd didn't "feel" born again, he accepted his friend's word by faith.

Shortly thereafter, Jack was walking through one of his drugstores and noticed copies of *Playboy* and *Penthouse* for sale in the magazine rack. He immediately called a meeting of his corporate officers and ordered that all sex magazines be removed from Eckerd drugstores nationwide. One of the officers questioned Eckerd's sanity and asked if he realized that his decision would cost him $3 million a year. Jack said his decision was final, and the purging of pornographic literature out of Eckerd drugstores was carried out. When Colson heard about all this, he was ecstatic. Eckerd simply replied to Colson's inquiry about the removal of the magazines, "God wouldn't let me off the hook."[8]

That's what happens when we turn our lives over to God. He doesn't let us off the hook. His Holy Spirit, magnifying the goodness and kindness of God, draws us to repentance (see Romans 2:4) and obedience. People may be amazed at Jack Eckerd's decision to give up $3 million of business, but he gained something far more valuable—a clear conscience before God. One of the greatest things we have to offer the world today is that marvelous freedom of a clear conscience. This gift of grace, purchased by the blood of Jesus, is one of the crown jewels of the Gospel. How amazing is the grace that not only saves us from the penalty of sin, but also breaks the power of sin over our lives!

STUDY GUIDE
CHAPTER 7

1) It is clear from Scripture that repentance is a necessary condition of salvation (see: Matthew 3:2, 4:17 ♦ Mark 1:15 ♦ Luke 13:3-5 ♦ Acts 2:38, 3:19, 17:30, 26:20 ♦ 2 Corinthians 7: 10 ♦ 2 Peter 3:9). Consider Bonhoeffer's description of "cheap grace" (pg. 62) and reflect on the need for true repentance.

2) In contrast to "cheap grace," meditate on Paul's description of one of the main functions of God's grace—to teach us how to live a lifestyle of repentance!

> For the grace of God that brings salvation has appeared to all men, teaching us that, denying ungodliness and worldly lusts, we should live soberly, righteously, and godly in the present age, looking for the blessed hope and glorious appearing of our great God and Savior Jesus Christ, who gave Himself for us, that He might redeem us from every lawless deed and purify for Himself His own special people, zealous for good works.
>
> —Titus 2:11-14

3) Nothing demonstrates the amazing grace and awesome goodness of God like the cross of Christ. Meditate on His sacrificial death along with Paul's declaration to the Romans that "The goodness of God leads us to repentance" (Romans 2: 4).

CHAPTER 8

The Good News in Person

I was converted in the 1970s during a move of God's Spirit that saw thousands of disillusioned hippie/surfer types like myself come to Christ. National magazines such as *Time*, *Look*, and *Life* featured pictures of hippie Christians with hands raised in worship during mass ocean baptisms that were commonplace back then. Lonnie Frisbee, one of the early counter-culture evangelists, actually led the *Look* magazine reporters to Christ when they came to interview him for an article on the Jesus Movement. I believe the reason there was so much good fruit from that movement is that the person of Jesus was honored above church traditions, denominations, and religious practices. We were called "Jesus People" or "Jesus Freaks," and we wore the titles gladly. I was once called a fool when I was preaching at an occult festival, and my response to the heckler was simply, "You're right, I'm a fool for Christ, but whose fool are you?"

The message of the Gospel rises or falls on the identity and accomplishments of Jesus of Nazareth. The claims that He made, the words that He said, and the accomplishment of His death and resurrection are unique in the annals of human history. It is not just a cute cliché to say, "Christianity is not a religion, but a relationship." It is *all about Jesus*!

Jesus—Unique as a Man

On many occasions, I have been accused of being a narrow-minded fundamentalist when it comes to my views about Jesus Christ. "How can you be so arrogant as to think that your way is the only way? How can you be so exclusive in a pluralistic society that has five major religions and thousands of minor ones?" As humbly as I can, I simply point them to the person of Jesus. I believe that Jesus is the only begotten Son of God. By definition, that excludes all others as a way of salvation.

C.S. Lewis, a Cambridge University professor and former agnostic, became one of Christianity's most articulate spokesman after his conversion. In his classic book, *Mere Christianity,* he writes regarding Jesus, "I am trying here to prevent anyone saying the really foolish thing that people often say about Him: 'I am ready to accept Jesus as a great moral teacher, but I don't accept His claim to be God.' That is one thing we must not say. A man who was merely a man and said the sort of things Jesus said would not be a great moral teacher. Either this man was and is the Son of God, or else a madman or something worse." Then Lewis adds, "You can shut Him up for a fool. You can spit at Him and kill Him as a demon, or you can fall at His feet and call Him Lord and God. But let us not come up with any patronizing nonsense about His being a great human teacher. He has not left that open to us. He did not intend to."[9] In other words, Lewis was simply saying that Jesus was a liar, a lunatic, or He was the Lord!

Jesus—Unique as a Messenger

While other religious teachers have made statements similar to those of Jesus, none have come close to the revolutionary nature of His teachings. Their variations of the Golden Rule, the Ten Commandments, and Christ's command to love one another inevitably require followers to adhere to a set of religious guidelines or practices. Jesus, however, taught that spiritual power comes through a personal relationship with God the Father. He spoke about hearing His Father's voice, doing the things that pleased His Father, and talked about God the Father in terms of moral character, not just natural attributes. This was as revolutionary in His day as it is in ours.

Jesus got beyond the outward observances of religious law (even His own Father's law) and got down to the heart of the matter. He focused attention on the intention of the Law rather than the outward observance of the Law. He spoke about hatred in the heart being the equivalent of murder and lust in the heart being the equivalent of adultery. Jesus was also unique in what He said about

Himself. He confirmed that He was the long-awaited Messiah and declared, "I am the way, the truth, and the life. No one comes to the Father except through Me" (John 14:6). What other spiritual leader has made such a claim? Not Mohammed, not Buddha, not Joseph Smith, or any other notable. Jesus was unique as a messenger because He was "the Word of God" in human form.

Jesus—Unique as a Miracle Worker

Through the centuries, there have been countless magicians, spiritists, and hucksters, but none has ever had the power of Jesus. He healed every sickness and every disease among the people (see Matthew 9:35). He cast out demons. He cleansed the lepers. He spoke prophetic words that changed people's lives. And most amazing of all, He raised people from the dead. The miracles of Jesus clearly affirm His spiritual authority.

Once after healing a paralytic, Jesus pronounced that the man's sins were forgiven. The scribes accused Jesus of blasphemy. Jesus, knowing their thoughts, said,

> Which is easier, to say, "Your sins are forgiven you," or to say, "Arise and walk"? But that you may know that the Son of Man has power on earth to forgive sins--then He said to the paralytic, "Arise, take up your bed, and go to your house."
>
> —Matthew 9:5-7

The obvious answer to His question was, "It's easier to *say*, 'Your sins are forgiven,'" than to actually heal a paralytic. Jesus linked His miracle-working power with His ability to forgive sins and used the healing as a demonstration. He still displays that awesome power to forgive sin and do miracles. For Jesus is the same yesterday, today, and forever (see Hebrews 13:8).

Jesus—Unique as the Messiah

Jesus not only predicted that He would die on the cross, but also that He would rise from the dead. His claim to be Israel's Messiah and the Savior of the world is either vindicated or disproved by these central facts.

That Jesus died is not disputed, even in secular, historical writings. The fact of His resurrection is what has been disputed. Josh McDowell, in his book, *More Than A Carpenter*, wrote that after 700 hours of studying the subject of the resurrection, "I came to the conclusion that the Resurrection of Jesus Christ is either one of the most wicked, vicious, heartless hoaxes ever foisted upon people, or it is the most important fact of history."[10] Paul the apostle declared to the Corinthians, "If Christ has not been raised, our preaching is useless and so is your faith" (1 Corinthians 15:14, NIV).

Various theories throughout history have been concocted to explain why the body of Jesus of Nazareth has never been found. One was the "wrong tomb" theory. This assumes that the women who reported the body of Christ missing had mistakenly gone to the wrong tomb. This means the disciples who went to check up on the women's statement must have also gone to the wrong tomb (along with the Roman guards, the angel, and the Jewish authorities!). If this were the case, why didn't the Romans or Jews produce the body to prove the disciples wrong?

Then there is the so-called "swoon" theory, which says that Jesus really didn't die. It claims that He merely fainted from exhaustion and loss of blood. A simple reading of the historical accounts about the horrors of crucifixion will render this theory most improbable. Can you imagine Jesus just walking off after being tortured, crucified, and lying for days in a tomb without food or water? No way!

A third theory popularized by the book *The Passover Plot* declares that the disciples stole the body of Jesus. This is even more improbable because it means the disciples would have died for what they knew to be a lie. Many people have given their lives for causes they believed in, but rarely have they willingly suffered death for something they knew to be false. Most of Jesus' disciples lived all of their lives in faithful obedience to Jesus Christ, living as if He had truly risen from the dead. And most of them died martyr's deaths, willingly sacrificing their lives for the risen Lord.

Dr. Simon Greenleaf, a Harvard professor and one of the greatest legal minds ever produced in this country, wrote a book entitled *The Testimony of the Evangelists: The Gospels Examined by the Rules of Evidence.* Greenleaf's conclusion was that the resurrection of Christ was one of the best-supported events in human history, according to the laws of legal evidence.[11]

Another lawyer, Frank Morison, set out to refute the evidence for the resurrection. But after honestly examining that evidence, he wrote a book called *Who Moved the Stone?*, which makes a strong case in favor of Christ's resurrection.[12] *Chicago Tribune* legal affairs reporter Lee Strobel also approached the claims of Christ as a confirmed skeptic. During his two years of study, he also became convinced by the evidence, and he recorded his findings in *The Case for Christ.*[13] The evidence confirms:

Jesus was unique as a man—He was God in the flesh (Colossians 2:9).

Jesus was unique as a messenger—He had the words of eternal life (John 6:68).

Jesus was unique as a miracle worker—His works testified to who He was (John 5:36).

Jesus was unique as the Messiah—He rose from the dead to prove who He was (Romans 1:4).

He is the Good News in person!

STUDY GUIDE
CHAPTER 8

1) In light of the fact that both Jesus and Paul predicted that false christs would seek to lead people away from the real Jesus (Matthew 24:5, 11, 24 ♦ 2 Corinthians 11:3-4), it is important for us to know from Scripture Who the real Jesus is. Study the following passages which reveal that Jesus is, in fact, God in human flesh:

   Isaiah 45:22 compare with **Philippians** 2:11 ♦ **Matthew** 1: 21-23 ♦ **John** 1:1, 1:14, 8:58, 10:30, 12:45, 14:6-10, 20:28-29 ♦ **Romans** 9:5 ♦ **2 Corinthians** 5:19 ♦ **Colossians** 1:15, 2:9 ♦ **1 Timothy** 3:16, 6:15-16 ♦ **Hebrews** 1:3-8 ♦ **1 John** 2:22-23, 4:1-3, 5:20 ♦ **Revelation** 1:8, 11, 17, 22:13-16.

2) One of the great challenges of world evangelization is to present Jesus in the midst of a world of religions. Consider these exclusive claims of Christ in an age of religious pluralism.

   John 6:27-69, 8:30-36, 58, 9:38-41, 10:1-10, 27-28, 11:25-27, 14:6 ♦ **Acts** 4:12 ♦ **Philippians** 2:5-11.

3) From the Old Testament sacrificial system to the ministry of John the Baptist to the Book of Revelation, Jesus is presented as "The Lamb of God who takes away the sin of the world!" (John 1:29). As a devotional exercise, meditate on what it cost God to provide for our salvation. It surely will help motivate you to a deeper commitment to evangelism.

CHAPTER 9

Saving Faith

Suppose you and some friends are sleeping on the second floor of an old mountain lodge during a church retreat. At 3 a.m., the smell of smoke and the light from the building going up in flames around you awakens you. Within seconds, you realize that all of your friends are in mortal danger. What is your response? If you really believe that the building is on fire, you will do whatever is necessary to get to safety and help your friends to do so as well. At that point, your concern is not whether your actions will disturb their sleep or appear as an overreaction. Your belief that the building is burning overcomes any obstacles in your mind and spurs your body to action.

This illustration highlights the issue of true faith. Many people believe that Jesus is the Son of God. For instance, in the United States, 80 percent of the population claims to be Christian. (Of these same folks, however, 70 percent had no clue what the term "John 3:16" meant, 90 percent could not define the Great Commission, and barely one-third knew the meaning of the word *Gospel*.)[14] What people do with their belief is what matters. The demons believe, and they tremble at His name (see James 2:19). At the end of the Sermon on the Mount, Jesus said that many will stand before Him at the judgment and tell of things they did in His name. To those He will say, "I never knew you; depart from Me, you who practice lawlessness!" (Matthew 7:23). Therefore, it's obviously possible to have a "said" faith rather than a "saving" faith.

Noted English author and theologian John Stott said, "The whole value of faith lies in its object (Jesus Christ), not in itself. Nevertheless, saving faith is not an 'acceptance of Jesus Christ as Savior' within a kind of mystical vacuum...Saving faith is a total penitent and submissive commitment to Christ..."[15]

Another good way to define saving faith is to look at what it is *not*. There are many commonly held beliefs that are not faith at all. By comparing them to Biblical standards, we can see just how solid that "faith" is. For example:

Faith is not an abstract "leap in the dark." It is not faith in faith. After my conversion, a friend said to me, "I'm happy for you, Danny. You needed something to believe in." I quickly realized that my friend didn't care whether I believed in Jesus or French toast for my salvation, as long as I believed in "something." But just believing in "something" will ultimately get you nothing. Saving faith always has as its object Jesus Christ and His Word.

Faith is not wishful or positive thinking. It is not visualizing good thoughts or having an optimistic personality. Faith is real. It is described in Hebrews 11:1 as being a *substance*, "the substance of things hoped for, the evidence of things not seen." This definition comes from a word that means, "that which stands under, or provides a basis for something else." Saving faith is solid—an active reality that we either have or don't have.

Faith is not a formula. In modern day evangelism, much has been made of the "sinner's prayer"—a formal, verbal statement to God of the acceptance of Jesus Christ as Savior and Lord. Although such prayers are often helpful for a person to "nail down" their commitment to Christ, the prayer itself does not save anyone. It is the commitment of our will to trust Jesus for our salvation—sinner's prayer or not—that truly saves. True, we must confess Jesus as our Lord, but this confession stands on a belief in the heart (see Romans 10:9-10).

Some Things We Must Believe

Saving faith requires that we fully embrace a few key facts about Jesus. These beliefs are essential because they are the foundation stones upon which we build our life in Christ. What are these core issues? The Apostle Paul clearly identifies them in two of his New Testament letters:

Now, brothers... hold firmly to the word I preached to you. Otherwise, you have believed in vain. For what I received I passed on to you as of first importance: that Christ died for our sins according to the Scriptures, that he was buried, that he was raised on the third day...and that he appeared to Peter, and then to the Twelve.

—1 Corinthians 15:1-5, NIV

...If you confess with your mouth, "Jesus is Lord," and believe in your heart that God raised him from the dead, you will be saved. For it is with your heart that you believe and are justified, and it is with your mouth that you confess and are saved.

—Romans 10:9-10, NIV

These "required" beliefs obviously revolve around the historical events of the death, burial, and resurrection of Jesus. Theologians call this the *kerygma* or *evangel*, both of which refer to a fixed body of truth that must be believed for people to actually be saved.

How Faith Comes

Again, we must understand that people come to saving faith in Jesus Christ through a growing response to God's initiatives of grace. This process is likened to the growth of plants, nurtured both by God and by man until they produce a harvest (see 1 Corinthians 3:6-9, Mark 4:26-29). Romans 10:17 also indicates a process when it says, "Faith *comes* by hearing, and hearing by the word of God" [emphasis mine]. We all have ears to hear spoken words, but only the Word of God can open the "ears" of our heart to truth. That often takes time.

The process of coming to saving faith also relates to four "wills" that are identified in 2 Timothy 2:24-26:

And the servant of the Lord must not strive; but be gentle unto all men, apt to teach, patient, in meekness instructing those that oppose themselves; if God peradventure will give them repentance to the acknowledging of the truth; and that they may recover themselves out of the snare of the devil, who are taken captive by his will (KJV).

The first will is that of the servant (Christian witness) who brings the Word. His humble approach with the Word can have a big impact on how it is received. The second is the will of the non-Christians who "oppose themselves" and hopefully will come to their senses and respond to the Word. The third will is the devil's. He is intent on keeping people enslaved to sin and blinded to the truth that will set them free. Finally, there is God's will. He is always present, ready to "give repentance" to anyone who turns to Him that they may escape from Satan's snare. For it is God's will that no person perish in his sin (see 2 Peter 3:9).

Though God wants all to embrace Him in faith, He never forces us to do so. As human beings created in His image, we have a free will to follow God or not. Christians who will exercise their wills to humbly present the Gospel and forcefully resist the devil can have a huge impact in the evangelism process. He gives us an active role in His work, aligning our will with His so that we can do battle against the forces of Satan and set captives free. The enduring mystery for the church is how this all works together to bring a person to saving faith.

Author A.W. Tozer once remarked concerning evangelism, that he prayed like a Calvinist (one who believes in predestination) and preached like an Arminian (one who believes in free will). To paraphrase, we need to pray as if it all depends on God and work as if it all depends on us. We would be wise to do the same, trusting God's promise, "So shall My word be that goes forth from My mouth; It shall not return to Me void, But it shall accomplish what I please, And it shall prosper in the thing for which I sent it" (Isaiah 55:11).

That moment when the Word finally works its way into the human heart and produces saving faith is one of amazing transformation. It's described by country music legend Hank

Williams in his classic song, "I Saw the Light." The song is aptly titled because saving faith takes us from darkness and death into the glorious light of the Savior's love.

> *I saw the Light, I saw the Light*
> *No more darkness, no more night*
> *Now I'm so happy, no sorrow in sight*
> *Praise the Lord, I saw the Light.*

STUDY GUIDE

CHAPTER 9

1) The main point of chapter 9 is to define what exactly constitutes the faith that saves. Jesus and other New Testament writers warned of a counterfeit faith that doesn't save (Matthew 7:21-27 ♦ 2 Corinthians 11:3-4 ♦ Galatians 1: 6-8 ♦ James 2:14-26 ♦ 1 John 2:4 ♦ Revelation 3:14-22). John Wesley called this faith "mental assent" as opposed to heart faith (Romans 10:9-10). The Bible even declares that the demons believe in Jesus (Mark 1:24 ♦ James 2:19). In your evangelistic message, consider how to lead people into true, saving faith.

2) Meditate on 1 Corinthians 15:1-4 and Ephesians 2:8-9 to discover what a person must believe and how a person comes to saving faith.

   See also: **John** 1:12, 3:16 ♦ **Acts** 16:31 ♦ **Romans** 3:23, 5:8, 10:9-10, 13 ♦ **Galatians** 2:16 ♦ **Hebrews** 11:1-6.

3) Many cults suggest there was a contradiction between Paul and James regarding the issue of saving faith saying that James added "works" to Paul's teaching on justification by faith (see Romans 4 and James 2:14-26). Study the following distinctions:

   a) Paul in Romans was combating a Jewish tendency of relying on obedience to the Law—an overemphasis on works. James was combating a kind of dead orthodoxy— an underemphasis on works.

b) Paul is speaking of works that <u>precede</u> faith as a means of salvation. James is speaking of works that follow a faith that alone saves.

c) Abraham was declared to be saved (justified) by faith in Genesis 15:6, which was 30 years before he offered Isaac on the altar. The Isaac situation (Genesis 22) demonstrated to all the faith by which he had already been justified.

d) Paul was making it clear that one "gets into" God's kingdom by faith. James insists God requires works from those who "are in." Faith must not be confused with works. Neither is faith separated from works.

CHAPTER 10

Our Future Home

Concepts like endless time, timeless eternity, and everlasting life seem to short-circuit our mental capacities. As we struggle to contemplate their meaning, our minds inevitably drift back to the nitty-gritty issues of the here and now. But even though we can never fully comprehend how awesome our eternal home in heaven will be, God has called us to live with a heavenly mindset.

James tells us that our present life is like a "mist that appears for a little while and then vanishes" (James 4:14, NIV). Therefore, the question of where we will spend eternity—in heaven or in hell—should be of huge importance to every human being.

We who want to live a lifestyle of evangelism must never forget that the hope of heaven is a central element of the Gospel message. It is the promise of Jesus that we who believe in His death and resurrection will rule and reign with Him for all eternity. Therefore, talking about heaven shouldn't be relegated to the lofty messages we preachers give to teary-eyed people at funerals. It should be proclaimed all the time as a joyous hope, a reminder that our present struggles will end one day, and a glorious future awaits us.

The Apostle Paul encouraged the Colossians to "set their affections on things above, not on things of the earth," and in an interesting play on words, he told the Corinthian Christians not to look at the things they could see, which were temporary, but at the invisible things, which were eternal (see Colossians 3:2; 2 Corinthians 4:18). Author C.S. Lewis put it this way, "Aim at heaven, and you get earth thrown in. Aim at earth and you get neither."[16] Because of the nature of our finite minds, it is impossible to *comprehend* heaven, but with the eyes of faith, we can *apprehend* it.

Many preachers today seem reluctant to preach on the subject of heaven thinking that we might become "so heavenly-minded that we are of no earthly good." I've often wondered who first made that statement because it is one of the most ludicrous and unscriptural things that a Christian could say. I would rather turn it around and say, "If you are not heavenly-minded, you won't be any earthly good!"

Heaven Waits

Scholars for years have debated the descriptions of heaven given in the Bible. Is the New Jerusalem literally 1,400 miles cubed? Is it really made of pure gold? Are the Pearly Gates for real? I'll leave those questions to the scholars. However, one image hits me as I read these mind-boggling descriptions of our future eternal home. I can picture an eternal magnifying glass that we receive by faith as we meditate on God's Word. In the Book of Revelation, John used the most valuable commodities known to man (gold, precious stones, pearls, etc.) to describe the things of heaven, trusting that readers would use that eternal "glass" to magnify them.

The Bible also describes heaven as a place where there will be no more death, tears, sorrow, or pain; in other words, eternal bliss! This again defies even the wildest imagination of our finite minds. If it is just perfect bliss, won't that in itself become perfectly boring? Isn't bliss itself more intensified by the sorrow, tension, or stress that preceded it? Isn't it more blissful to win a game in sudden-death overtime than it is to win a blowout? Won't anything eternal, even if it is joy, get monotonous and absolutely maddening? Wouldn't even Tiger Woods be bored after just one day of consecutive holes-in-one?

The answer is found in the character of God. Because God is there, heaven will be anything but boring. Since He created all the things that bring us love and joy and pleasure here on Earth, just imagine what He has done with heaven. I think that God gives us little tastes of it just so we can get a tiny glimpse of heaven. To help you get such a glimpse, think of some moment in your life when you simply could do nothing but clench your fists in triumph and exclaim, "YES!!! It doesn't get any better than this!" Here's my image of such a moment (you can substitute yours).

I'm paddling out on my surfboard on a glassy ocean near sunset as a six-foot swell is peaking on the South Shore of Oahu. Out with just a few friends, I sniff the salt air and gaze out on translucent blue-green waves, pumping out in tubular cylinders of perfect artistic harmony. Near the horizon, a yellow-orange sun is changing colors by the moment as the light dances on the clouds. I take off on a wave, turn at the bottom, smack the lip of the wave, then stall and scream with incredible speed into the womb of a wave that seems created just for that moment and me. Swallowed up for a few seconds, seemingly buried under a wall of white water, I am spit out at the other end still standing. And with clenched fists, I shout to the sky, "YES !!! It doesn't get any better than this!"

Then with my heavenly magnifying glass, I multiply that experience a couple of million times and sing with my friend Keith Green (who now resides in heaven):

> *I can't wait to get to heaven*
> *When you'll wipe away all my tears*
> *In six days you created everything*
> *But you've been workin' on heaven 2,000 years.*[17]

A Scratch in the Sand of Time

What's most incredible to me as I think about heaven is that its joys and pleasures will go on without limit. We live in a world bound by time. Everything is measured in seconds, minutes, hours, days, weeks, months, years, and so on. The "sting of death" unfortunately ensures that golfers like Tiger Woods will one day play their last game and surfers like me will ride their last wave. All of us have a date with the undertaker. The certainty of death is still 100 percent. The indescribable, glorious, unfathomable truth is that "death has lost its sting and the grave is no longer our conqueror" (see 1 Corinthians 15:55). WE ARE GOING TO LIVE FOREVER, dear reader. Let me hear you shout AMEN!!!

I live just three miles from the most famous beach in the world. Waikiki Beach in Honolulu is two miles of gorgeous white sand with palm trees blowing in the trade winds and "sky shows" every night at sunset that render any artist jealous with envy. I like to go there occasionally just to run my fingers and toes through its silky sand. As I do, I sometimes try to imagine a seagull picking up a grain of sand, flying to California, depositing it there, and then flying back, picking up another grain of sand, and repeating this procedure. When Waikiki has been emptied of the multiple quadrillions of grains of sand by this one seagull, the first day of eternity has just begun!

My friend, Pastor Wayne Cordeiro, gives the following illustration: "Suppose somehow you are able to fire an arrow from here on the earth all the way to the moon. Then suppose someone on the moon was able to grab the rope that was attached to the end of the arrow and pull it very taut between your location and the moon. Somewhere along the rope you take a No. 2 pencil and you etch a tiny scratch the width of the pencil lead on the rope that has been fired to the moon. That is what our lives are like compared to eternity. Unfortunately, so many of us live our lives for the 'scratch' and not for the length of the rope."

King David once prayed, "Lord, make me to know my end and to appreciate the measure of my days—what it is; let me know and realize how frail I am [how transient is my stay here]. Behold, You have made my days as handbreadths, and my lifetime is as nothing in Your sight. Truly every man at his best is merely a breath!" (Psalm 39:4-6, Amplified). We should capitalize on the desire that God put in everyone to know what happens after death. It seems that in every culture—from the ancient Egyptians with their mummies to the modern mystics—there is a deep concern about the afterlife. The closer people get to their own physical death, the more concerned they become about it. We who have no fear of the afterlife can bring hope to those who do. Paul wrote to the Thessalonians, "But I do not want you to be ignorant, brethren, concerning those who have fallen asleep, lest you sorrow as others who have no hope" (1 Thessalonians 4:13). Certainly, a part of our good news is our great God has created an eternal dwelling place where we can spend forever with Him.

Few realize that John and Charles Wesley, the famous founders of the Methodist movement, began their preaching careers as dismal failures as missionaries to Georgia, one of America's new colonies. The chief reason being that they were not saved! The emptiness of their professing Christianity was heightened by their terror when the ship that was transporting them back to England encountered a squall that nearly sank it. In the midst of their fear, they noticed a group of Moravians in another part of the ship calmly singing hymns. When the ship was out of the bad weather, the brothers inquired of the Moravians how they could be so calm. They simply said, "We know that when we die we are assured of going to heaven." The Wesleys knew that with all their religious rituals, they lacked that assurance. Shortly thereafter, they were soundly saved, and the rest is history.[18]

Paul the apostle longed to be in that eternal dwelling place. To the Philippians, he said in so many words, "I want to die and go to heaven, but since you need me, I'll hang around for awhile!" He described us as being in a period of intense "groaning" while we are in these bodies waiting to go to heaven (see Philippians 1:21 and 2 Corinthians 5:2). Did he have some sort of a morbid death wish or a disdain for life? I think not. I simply think he had an accurate evaluation of time compared with eternity and was homesick for heaven. We should be homesick for it too.

STUDY GUIDE
CHAPTER 10

1) "Do not lay up for yourselves treasures on earth, where moth and rust destroy and where thieves break in and steal; but lay up for yourselves treasures in heaven, where neither moth nor rust destroys and where thieves do not break in and steal. For where your treasure is, there your heart will be also" (Matthew 6:19-21).

Jesus specifically commanded us to do two things with regards to "treasure"—that which we value: don't lay up treasures on earth; and lay up treasures in heaven. He then gives four reasons to obey this double command:

a) Treasures on earth are temporary.

b) Treasures on earth are corruptible.

c) Treasures on earth are vulnerable to theft.

d) Where we lay up our treasures helps us discover where our heart really is.

In light of this command, take an inventory of where you spend your treasures, time, and talents. Do they reflect eternal or temporal values and treasures? How does this affect your zeal for evangelism and help others get their focus on eternity?

2) Jesus said, "For what profit is it to a man if he gains the whole world, and loses his own soul? Or what will a man give in exchange for his soul?" (Matthew 16:26).

In these two rhetorical questions, Jesus is pointing out the value of a human soul. The obvious conclusion He wants us to reach is that a human being is of more value than all the things that could potentially "profit" a person on the earth simply because we are eternal beings. Meditate on these two questions, and let God's perspective on the lost people in the world intensify your zeal for evangelism.

3) Paul opened his second letter to the Corinthians talking to them about the pressures that surrounded his ministry of evangelism to the point of saying he, "...despaired even of life" (2 Corinthians 1:8). In the fourth chapter, he went on to describe what kept him from "giving up" (2 Corinthians 4: 1,16): "While we do not look at the things which are seen, but at the things which are not seen. For the things which are seen are temporary, but the things which are not seen are eternal" (2 Corinthians 4:18).

Reflect on Paul's eternal perspective whenever you are tempted to "give up" in your lifestyle of evangelism.

See: **Mark** 8:36 ♦ **Luke** 9:25, 10:20, 20:34-38 ♦ **John** 5:24, 8: 52, 11:26, 14:2 ♦ **Acts** 7:55-56 ♦ **Romans** 2:7 ♦ **1 Corinthians** 15:51-58 ♦ **2 Corinthians** 5:1-11 ♦ **Philippians** 1:21, 3:20-21 ♦ **Colossians** 1:13 ♦ **2 Timothy** 1:10 ♦ **Titus** 1:2 ♦ **Hebrews** 11:10 ♦ **James** 5:20 ♦ **1 Peter** 1:4 ♦ **Revelation** 4, 5, 22:14.

SECTION III

The Motives for Sharing the Good News

One of our greatest privileges as human beings is that we bear the imprint of our Maker. We are created in the image of God, and a key aspect of this image is volition or free choice. This is what separates us from the rest of creation. God could have created us to simply follow animal instincts. He also could have created us as robotic automatons to fulfill His will. Instead, He "took a chance" and gave us this aspect of His own nature. He chose to do so because He knew that the deepest relationships form only when free choice is involved.

One of the reasons we study God's character is that we see how aspects of His character (love, kindness, goodness, faithfulness, etc.) *motivate Him* to take certain actions. For example, "...God so loved the world *that He gave*..." (John 3:16, emphasis mine). This great verse shows that He gave His Son as an atoning sacrifice for our sins out of a motive of love for us.

Having strong motives also drives the work of evangelism. In this section, we will examine what I believe are the five strongest motives for personal and corporate evangelism. If believers will let the Holy Spirit fully apply these motives, they will spark in us a desire to go and keep going until we have reached the whole world for Christ.

The first and most powerful of these is love. However, the other four motives are also very important. They include obedience to Christ, compassion for the lost, recognition of the shortness of the time, and a desire to help others experience abundant life in Christ. When we understand the "why" of going, we will be further convinced of the need and the urgency to start reaching out ever farther with the love of Jesus.

THE MOTIVES

Evangelistic Motives	Biblical Principle	Evangelistic Focus	Bottom Line	Relevant Scripture
Love of God	Without Love we are nothing	Obey the Great Commandment	Concern	(Matthew 22:37-40 ◆ 1 Corinthians 13)
Lordship of Christ	Jesus is Lord - He told us to GO!	Obey the Great Commission	Commitment	(Mark 16:15 ◆ Matthew 28:19-20)
Lostness of Man	The wages of sin is death	Warn of God's judgment	Compassion	(Romans 6:23 ◆ 2 Corinthians 5:11)
Last Days	We must work while it is day. The night is coming.	Follow God's urgency	Compulsion	(John 9:4 ◆ Romans 13: 12)
Life of Jesus	What would Jesus Do?	Live Jesus' Example	Character	(John 10:10, 13:14)

CHAPTER 11

Motive #1: Love

For Christ's love compels us, because we are convinced
that one died for all, and therefore all died.

—2 Corinthians 5:14, NIV

In the summer of 1999, people across America were astonished
by the dramatic story of three rock climbers in Yosemite National
Park. Peter Terbush, Kerry Pyle, and Joe Kerwin were climbing a
sheer cliff in the majestic central California park when, without
warning, a section of the wall above them started to collapse. Tons
of rock began sliding toward the three climbers. Remarkably, one
slab of rock wedged against the rope held by Terbush. In that
moment, he faced a terrifying decision. He could pull himself to
safety and let the rocks fall on his friends below, or he could hold
on as long as possible, giving his fellow climbers precious seconds
to flee to safety. Terbush chose to hold the rope. Later on that day,
Pyle and Kerwin described to the news media how their friend had
literally laid his life down for them. Only after his friends were a
safe distance away, did Terbush attempt to get out from under the
rocks before they fell. He was unsuccessful and was buried under
the rubble. His two friends are eternally grateful, but unfortunately,
they did not have the opportunity to thank him.[19]

Throughout the ages, courageous men and women have made
similar sacrifices for people they loved or causes they believed in.
Their sacrifices for earthly kingdoms, temporal relationships, or
fleeting moments of fame and glory are noble. But how much more
noble is the motive to save people from an eternal separation from
the One who created us and made the ultimate sacrifice so that we
could be with Him for all eternity?

There is simply no greater motive for evangelism than a deep
love for God. A passion for souls begins with a passion for God. As

we fall deeper in love with the God who first loved us (see 1 John 4:19), His love and concern for the rest of the world just naturally rubs off on us. Such love will cause us to make any sacrifice, bear any burden, and suffer any hardship for the sake of pleasing the One we love. We see this illustrated in temporal love affairs every day on a smaller scale. On the largest scale, we see it in the motivation that God had to send His Son into the world to die for us. "But God demonstrates His own love toward us, in that while we were still sinners, Christ died for us" (Romans 5:8).

A passionate pursuit of the love of God and a desperate desire to see Him glorified and honored will keep the flames of evangelism burning hot in our soul, even when our compassion for people, our awareness of the last days, or our perspective on heaven and hell grows dim. The questions we need to continually ask ourselves when we grow cold towards the lost are: Do I love the Lord with all my heart? Do I desire to please Him? Do I want to make His heart glad? He gave us a glimpse into His heart when He let us peek at a heavenly scene. "…there will be more joy in heaven over one sinner who repents than over ninety-nine just persons who need no repentance" (Luke 15:7).

All You Need Is Love/Love is All You Need

There is no fear in love; but perfect love casts out fear, because fear involves torment. But he who fears has not been made perfect in love.

—1 John 4:18

John, the apostle of love, recognized that the fear of man was a serious obstacle to evangelism, so he defined the problem in a rather mathematical way: the degree to which we increase in love is the degree to which we decrease in fear.

I saw clearly how love could overcome fear in the case of a young mother named Healani. Though she had grown up in Hawaii, Healani was fearful of many things that live there, particularly the insects and rodents. Whenever a mouse or a cockroach came into her kitchen, she would shriek and jump up on a chair in fear of these harmless creatures. However, when a pit bull started charging at her two-year-old son, Corey, while they were at a local park, Healani did not hesitate for a moment. She jumped between Corey and the snarling attack dog, grabbed him by the jaws, and threw him away from her precious baby. The pit bull fled with its tail between its legs. How remarkable that a woman who is petrified of harmless insects would stand up to a vicious pit bull. She willingly put herself in harm's way out of love for her son. Her "perfect love cast out" her fear.

A passionate love for God will help us overcome all kinds of fears. Peter was a man who had fears like ours, but he overcame them through love and obedience to Christ. He was afraid to step out of the boat and walk upon the waves, but he did so when Jesus said to come (see Matthew 14:22-31). He was afraid to fellowship with non-Jews, but he did so when Jesus told him to go (see Acts 10). And he was afraid to speak publicly, but he preached boldly when the Holy Spirit came upon him in Jerusalem. Peter's love for the Lord compelled him to obedience, and thousands of people were won to Christ (see Acts 2).

Another important aspect of this issue is our determination to abide in the Lord's love. All of us are born with a need for love and acceptance. If we do not receive our love and acceptance from our Heavenly Father, we will seek it somewhere else, often from the very people to whom we are trying to witness. That road ultimately leads to unbelief, fear, and frustration.

To be "in Christ" is to be fully secure in His love, recognizing and accepting that He loves us not because of what we've done, but because of His grace. It also means that we are more concerned with pleasing God than with pleasing people. Most Christians who struggle with fear related to personal evangelism simply care more about what people think of them than what God thinks of them. This is why Paul encouraged the Ephesians "to know the love of Christ which passes knowledge, that you might be filled with all the fullness of God" (Ephesians 3:18-19). Even though it cannot be comprehended, except by revelation of the Spirit of God, His love is wider, longer, deeper, and higher than any other type of love we can experience. When we are secure in that love, the fear of man will be cast out.

Speaking the Truth in Love

In addition to our love for God as a motive, there is also the need to love the people we are seeking to win for Christ. A true friend is someone who loves you enough to tell you the truth. You may not like what they have to say at the time, but if you honestly consider their words, you are usually grateful later on. Paul instructed us to "speak the truth in love" (see Ephesians 4:15), knowing that it would not only bring more people into the church, but also make it a healthier one.

I was recently told by a friend who had been diagnosed with cancer about the straightforward "advice" his doctor gave him. Upon hearing his diagnosis, my friend made light of the doctor's original counsel to get an operation. Instead, he said he was going to experiment with various homespun remedies. The doctor looked him in the eye and said, "If you do not have this operation, you will die!" The sternness of the doctor's voice, the compassion on his face, and the authority of his years in the medical profession persuaded my friend to get the operation, and today he is cured. If the doctor would have smiled, hugged my friend and said, "I love you," and not told him the truth, most likely my friend would be dead now. I think that would have been wrong and possibly even criminal.

When skeptics confront me about the urgency I place on preaching the Gospel, I usually respond by saying, "If you were a researcher at the Mayo Clinic and you discovered the cure for AIDS, would you keep it to yourself? If you were a doctor for the American Cancer Society and came up with a cure for cancer, would it be loving or wise to keep the information private?" The answer is obvious. The spiritual parallel is that we have the cure to something much worse than AIDS or cancer. The world is deathly sick with a disease called sin. Love demands that we overcome the fear of man and tell people the truth of the Gospel.

This also applies to those of us who promote what is called "friendship evangelism." It goes without saying that we should be friendly and kind towards people we are trying to win to Christ. However, we must remember that "friendship" is the adjective and "evangelism" is the noun describing what we are to do when we go into the world. That is, we are to *evangelize*. Love and friendship describe the way we are to evangelize, but they do not replace the evangelism. Friendship is a supplement to evangelism, not a substitute for evangelism. I am all for building bridges of love and friendship to non-Christians, but we must be sure that we cross those bridges once we build them! I do not want to stand before God on Judgment Day and have non-Christians say to the Lord, "Danny loved me, respected my dignity as a human being, and showed his love for me in many ways, but he never told me that I was a sinner, separated from God, and in need of God's forgiveness." The simple love that we have for people will dictate our response in sharing the Gospel with them. If we do not pray for them and seek to share the Gospel with them, I seriously doubt whether we really love them as God requires.

STUDY GUIDE
CHAPTER 11

1) In Paul's famous "love chapter", 1 Corinthians 13, he sandwiches some incredibly strong teaching on love between a chapter detailing spiritual gifts (chapter 12) and their orderly exercise (chapter 14).

    a) First, consider the seven types of Christians he mentions in vs. 1-3. See which one you most identify with and feel the weight of the word "nothing", which describes the value of all our virtues if we don't have love.

        i) "I speak with the tongues of men and angels"—"Charismatic" Christians

        ii) "I have the gift of prophecy"—"Prophetic" Christians

        iii) "Understand all mysteries"—"Mystical" Christians

        iv) "Have all knowledge"——"Student" Christians

        v) "I have all faith"——"Faith" Christians

        vi) "I give all my possessions to the poor"—"Activist" Christians

        vii) "I give my body to be burned"—"Sacrificial" Christians

If I have not love, I am nothing!

    b) Secondly, consider the 16 characteristics by which we can identify love in our lives (vs. 4-8), and then take personal inventory on how these things are present or absent in our attitudes in evangelism.

        i) Patient

ii) Kind

iii) Not envious

iv) Not boastful

v) Not proud

vi) Not rude

vii) Not self-seeking

viii) Not angry

ix) Keeps no record of wrong

x) Doesn't rejoice in evil

xi) Rejoices in truth

xii) Always protects

xiii) Always trusts

xiv) Always hopes

xv) Always perseveres

xvi) *LOVE NEVER FAILS!*

(Pastor Chuck Smith gives the suggestion when reading this chapter to substitute your name for love every time you see it in the passage, then substitute the name Jesus Christ in the same way.) Compare and contrast.

2) Meditate on John 3:16. Substitute the name of the people you are praying for to become Christians. Let the revelation of God's incredible love for them stir you to a deeper prayer life and more boldness in witnessing.

3) Paul wrote to the Corinthians about God's love as the primary factor in his motivation to live for the Lord and the salvation of the lost:

> For the love of Christ constraineth [controls] us;
> because we thus judge, that if one died for all, then
> were all dead: And that he died for all, that they which
> live should not henceforth live unto themselves, but
> unto him which died for them, and rose again.
>
> —2 Corinthians 5:14-15, KJV

He then went on to describe our evangelistic ministry as
"ambassadors for Christ" (v. 20). Knowing that an ambassador
is a representative of his country, examine your own motive for
evangelism in light of the fact that we are representing a God
of love (1 John 4:16).

CHAPTER 12
Motive #2: Lordship

Upon the death of Princess Diana in 1997, there was much discussion about her son, Prince William, becoming the future King of England. Even though he is immensely popular and will most likely eclipse the popularity of his father on the day he is crowned, Prince William will nonetheless be a figurehead leader. You see, in the United Kingdom, the real authority to "call the shots" no longer rests in the hands of the king, but with the prime minister. The king may voice his views and represent the nation at state events, but it is the prime minister who ultimately decides whether England will go to war, continue its NATO Alliance, or take a stand for or against Israel.

As we begin the 21st century, I fear that our understanding of the words "Lord and King" is far different from those of New Testament Christians. The kings in Jesus' time were powerful rulers. "Lord" in the New Testament is translated from the Greek word *kurios*, a title that Julius Caesar applied to himself in 44 B.C. In the Gentile mind of the day, it meant "ruler" or "despot". The Jews got a lecture on Christ's supreme authority when Peter declared at Pentecost, "Let all the house of Israel know assuredly that God has made this Jesus, whom you crucified, both Lord [kurios] and Christ [Messiah]" (Acts 2:36). Lord was the word for the civil ruler and Christ or Messiah was the word for Savior.

In giving us the Great Commission, Jesus said, "All authority has been given to Me in heaven and on earth" (Matthew 28:18). In other words, Jesus has the right to rule. And because He has the right to rule, He has the authority to call the shots. And the last shot that He called before He ascended into heaven was, "Go into all the world and preach the gospel to every creature" (Mark 16:15).

One of our highest motives for a lifestyle of evangelism should simply be because Jesus is the Lord, and He told us to do it. The

Great Commission is not the "Great Suggestion" or the "Great Option." The authority of the Lord to command those subjects under His rule was understood clearly in Biblical times. This underscores Peter's lame reply to Jesus when he was commanded by the resurrected Christ to "rise, kill, and eat" the animals that were within the sheet in his vision on Simon's housetop. It was a visual picture of God's desire for him to preach the Gospel to the Gentiles (see Acts 10:9-13). Peter's reply was, "Not so, Lord!" You just don't say "no" to someone who is your Lord!

Jesus has clearly given a commandment, an irrevocable mandate to us as His disciples, to take the Gospel to "the uttermost parts of the earth" (see Acts 1:8). A casual reading of the Book of Acts shows the clear understanding the disciples had of Jesus' statement, "make disciples of all nations" (Matthew 28: 19). Paul the apostle carried it on in his teaching in his letters, "For we do not preach ourselves, but Christ Jesus the Lord, and ourselves your bondservants for Jesus' sake" (2 Corinthians 4:5). Paul instructed Timothy to "Preach the word! Be instant in season and out of season ...do the work of an evangelist, make full proof of your ministry" (see 2 Timothy 4:2,5). The early apostles and their followers knew that they were accountable to Jesus as Lord, and He had bidden them to proclaim the good news to all the world. How could they face Him unashamed if they had flouted His last command?

Disciples of Jesus understand that obedience is not an option for them. "Then Jesus said to those Jews who believed Him, 'If you abide in My word, you are My disciples indeed. And you shall know the truth, and the truth shall make you free'" (John 8:31-32). The freedom that is promised along *with the truth* is tied to obedience *to the truth*. Therefore, we should come up with strategies of prayer, planning, and preaching that will most adequately and effectively fulfill the command of Christ to make disciples of all nations.

Robert Coleman starts out his classic book, *The Master Plan of Evangelism*, with the following challenge:

This is a question that should be posed continually in relation to the evangelistic activities in the church. Are our efforts to keep things going fulfilling the Great Commission of Christ? Do we see an ever-expanding company of dedicated men reaching the world with the Gospel as a result of our ministry? That we are busy in the church trying to work one program after another cannot be denied. But are we accomplishing our objectives?[20]

The people of God need to rise up and see themselves as not only sons or daughters in God's family, but as soldiers in His army. As such, we have been commanded to fight for the souls of men and the nations of the world. We have no option to accept Christ without accepting His demands. A disciple of Jesus is by definition someone who has given Jesus authority over his life. Jesus is the King of kings. He is the Lord of lords. He is the Captain of our Salvation. And He has given us a job to do, a task to perform. If we are truly obedient disciples of Jesus Christ, we will do it.

As the late evangelist Leonard Ravenhill said, we should "pray as if it all depended on God and work as if it all depended on us" until that glorious day when we have reached every creature with the Gospel, or until Jesus Christ comes back, whichever comes first.

In fact, we should go into the world and preach the Gospel to every person even if no one responds! Why? Simply because Jesus is the Lord and He told us to. Jesus said, "If you love Me, keep My commandments" (John 14:15). And "You are My friends if you do whatever I command you" (John 15:14). His last command was to Go. Let's Go!

In one of the last songs that Keith Green wrote before he went to be with the Lord, he penned these words:

> *Jesus commands us to go,*
> *It should be the exception if we stay.*
> *It's no wonder we're moving so slow*

> *When His children refuse to obey,*
> *Feeling so called to stay.*[21]

The earliest baptismal confession recorded in the annals of church history records that just before a person was dipped in the waters of baptism, he proclaimed simply, "Kurios Jesus"—"Jesus is Lord." May we not only confess it, but also live it out as we obey His last command.

STUDY GUIDE
CHAPTER 12

1) Several word pictures are given to us in the New Testament to describe the church. In Ephesians we are likened to a body (1: 23), a temple (2:20-22), a family (3:15), and a bride (5:22-23).

In chapter 6, however, Paul switches to a military metaphor. We are also an army. Christ is not only the head of the body, builder of the temple, head of the family, and husband of the bride, but He is also the commander-in-chief of God's army. Consider not only the Old Testament military campaigns as examples, but also these New Testament Scriptures as insights into our identity as soldiers and the nature of our war:

See: **Romans** 7:23, 13:12 ♦ **1 Corinthians** 15:24 ♦ **2 Corinthians** 10:3-6 ♦ **Ephesians** 6:10-20 ♦ **1 Timothy** 1:18, 6: 12 ♦ **2 Timothy** 2:1-4 ♦ **Hebrews** 10:32 ♦ **James** 4:7 ♦ **1 Peter** 5:8 ♦ **Revelation** 3:21, 6:2, 12:11, 17:14.

2) As our Lord (absolute ruler, commander-in-chief), Jesus commanded us to make disciples by teaching all nations to obey all of His commands (Matthew 28:18-20). Consider some of these "commands of Christ," and measure your obedience to the Great Commission.

   a) Repentance (Matthew 4:17 ♦ Mark 1:15 ♦ Luke 13:3-5, 24:47)
   b) Faith (John 6:25-29)
   c) Love God and neighbor (Matthew 22:37-39 ♦ Mark 12: 30-31 ♦ Luke 10:27)
   d) Servanthood (John 13:1-17)

e) Forgiveness (Matthew 6:14-15)

f) The Lord's Supper (Luke 22:19)

g) Love one another (John 13:34-35)

h) Obedience (John 8:31, 14:15, 21, 15:10)

i) Fruit-bearing (John 15:8)

j) World evangelism (Mark 16:15 ♦ Luke 24:47 ♦ Acts 10: 42)

k) Making disciples (Matthew 28:18-20 ♦ John 20:21)

3) Paul summed up his evangelistic ministry to the Corinthians with a two-fold description, "For we do not preach ourselves, but Christ Jesus the Lord, and ourselves your bondservants for Jesus' sake" (2 Corinthians 4:5):

a) His message—The Lordship of Christ

b) His example—Servanthood

Consider practical ways we can proclaim the Lordship of Christ (His claims on every area of a person's life) with a humble attitude of serving the people we are seeking to convert to Christ.

CHAPTER 13

Motive #3: The Lostness of the Lost

It is said that William Booth, founder of the Salvation Army, wished all his officers could hang over hell for 24 hours prior to their commissioning. He felt sure this would stir them to a deeper commitment to evangelism. While a greater awareness of hell and the lostness of men should perhaps not be our primary motive for evangelism, knowing that we are delivered from the wrath to come should have a definite place in our motivation for missions (see 1 Thessalonians 1:9-10).

The Bible gives some rather hideous word pictures regarding the eternal state of people who have died without Christ. Jesus spoke of an eternal abode of the lost, describing it as a place of "everlasting punishment" and "outer darkness" where there is "weeping and gnashing of teeth" (Matthew 8:12, 25:46). Peter spoke of a "mist of darkness ... reserved forever" for false teachers, and Jude spoke of the "blackness of darkness forever" (2 Peter 2:17; Jude 13). In light of such descriptions, it would serve us well to meditate on the subject of hell and allow God to break our hearts with the very thing that breaks His heart—the thousands of souls that pass away every day into a Christ-less eternity.

Charles Spurgeon, the Prince of Preachers, is not known for "hellfire and brimstone" sermons, but in one instance, he sought to bring a greater awareness of hell to his hearers. He said,

> We have never seen the invisible things of horror. That land of terror is a land unknown. God has put somewhere, on the edge of His dominion, a fearful lake that burns with fire and brimstone...your body will be prepared by God in such a way that it will burn forever without being consumed, with your nerves laid raw by the searing flame, yet never desensitized for all its raging fury and acrid smoke of the sulfurous flames searing your lungs and choking your breath. You will cry out for the mercy of death, but it will never, no never, no never give you rest.[22]

Jonathan Edwards, in his epic sermon, *Sinners in the Hands of an Angry God*, said,

Oh, sinner, consider the fearful danger you are in! It is a great furnace of anger, a wide and bottomless pit, full of the fire of wrath that you are held over in the hand of that God whose wrath has provoked and incensed as much against you as against many of the damned in hell. You hang by a slender thread, with the flames of divine wrath flashing about it and ready any moment to singe it and burn it asunder; and you have no interest in any mediator, and nothing to lay hold of to save yourself, nothing to keep you off the flames of wrath, nothing of your own, nothing that you have ever done, nothing that you can do to induce God to spare you one moment.[23]

Ouch!

Theologians and Bible teachers have been debating for years on the particulars about hell. Is it really hot, and if so, how hot is it? If it's a lake of fire, how can there be darkness? If fire by nature is a physical property, how can it exist in a spiritual state, burning souls which are by nature spiritual? If hell is truly everlasting, how can a God of justice invoke an everlasting punishment for temporal sin? These are questions that we will not attempt to answer here, except to say that whatever hell is, men and women without Christ will go there and will never again have a chance to live eternally in the presence of God. This alone should fill us with a sense of horror as to the state of lost human beings.

This work of evangelism is serious business. We are not just trying to give people a new lease on life by joining our religion. We are dealing with the issues of life or death and heaven or hell every time we encounter a non-believer. Paul spoke of having unceasing grief in his heart and wishing he were cursed from Christ for the sake of the lost (see Romans 9:2-3). The Psalmist also agonized in his concern for the lost: "Horror has taken hold upon me because of the wicked that forsake thy law ... rivers of waters run down mine eyes" (see Psalm 119:53,136). Jeremiah spoke of bitterly weeping over the pride of his people (see Jeremiah 13:17). Many of us find these descriptions of hell and the responses of Paul, David, and Jeremiah perhaps to be eccentric or extreme, but how can we say they are extreme in the light of the reality of hell? If only God would give us half the revelation of the lostness of the lost that these men had, we would be led to fasting, prayer, spiritual warfare, giving, and fearless witnessing to see the lost come to Jesus so that they might escape the dangers of a Christ-less eternity.

Leonard Ravenhill tells of Charlie Peace, a convicted criminal sentenced to die by hanging. On his death walk to the gallows, the prison chaplain glibly read to Charlie some Bible verses from a book called, *The Consolations of Religion*. Charlie was shocked that a minister who professed to believe in the Bible could so coldly and professionally read about hell without so much as a tear in his eye or a quiver in his voice. "How can he believe that there is an eternal fire that never consumes its victims and yet be so unmoved?" Charlie mused to himself. Finally, unable to hold his peace any longer, the convict snapped at the chaplain, "Sir, if I believed what you and the church of God say you believe, even if England were covered with broken glass from coast to coast, I would walk over it, if need be, on hands and knees and think it worthwhile living just to save one soul from an eternal hell like that."[24] Charlie spent his last moments on earth with a passionless, unbelieving preacher and went on to spend his eternity in hell.

Paul said he had the "spirit of faith, according to what is written, 'I believed, therefore I spoke,' we also believe and therefore speak" (2 Corinthians 4:13). It follows, then, that if we truly believe the Gospel is God's absolute, final word to mankind regarding salvation, our only proper response should be to get the good news out by all means possible. After declaring that we must all stand before the judgment seat of Christ, Paul declares, "Knowing, therefore, the terror of the Lord, we persuade men" (2 Corinthians 5:11).

I'm not necessarily advocating that we incorporate hell more into our witnessing to the lost, although it may be appropriate at times. However, my point is that we Christians who know the "terror of the Lord" should be motivated to persuade men.

STUDY GUIDE
CHAPTER 13

1) The Bible's teaching on hell (mostly coming from Jesus Himself) focuses on two aspects of this awful place originally "prepared for the devil and his angels" (Matthew 25:41)—its eternity and its severity. Meditate on the following descriptions of hell, and identify with a brokenhearted God who, although He created Hell, has "no pleasure in the death of the wicked" (Ezekiel 33:11) and "is not willing that any should perish" (2 Peter 3:9).

a) Hell is eternal:

o Daniel 12:2—"Everlasting contempt."

o Matthew 3:12 ♦ Luke 3:17—"Unquenchable fire."

o Mark 9:38-43—"Unquenchable fire where their worm dieth not and the fire is not quenched."

o Matthew 18:8—"Everlasting fire."

o Matthew 10:28—"Fear Him who can destroy both soul and body in hell."

o Matthew 25:46—"Everlasting punishment."

o Mark 3:29—"Everlasting damnation."

o 2 Thessalonians 1:9—"Everlasting destruction."

o Hebrews 6:1-7—"Eternal judgment."

o 2 Peter 2:17—"The mist of darkness reserved forever."

o Jude 13—"Blackness of darkness forever."

o Revelation 20:15—"The lake of fire."

b) Hell is severe:

- o   Matthew 5:29-30—Better to lose a hand or an eye than to go to hell.
- o   Matthew 7:23—Separated from the presence of Christ.
- o   Matthew 8:12—Outer darkness; there will be weeping and gnashing of teeth.
- o   Matthew 10:28—Destruction.
- o   Matthew 25:41—Punishment.
- o   Matthew 12:32—No forgiveness.
- o   Luke 16:19-31—No second chance.
- o   Romans 2:8—Indignation and wrath.
- o   Revelation 21:8—The lake which burns with fire and brimstone.

2)   Paul spoke of the "terror of the Lord" being a motivating factor in helping him to "persuade men" (2 Corinthians 5:11). While the fear of hell is never used in the Bible as a threat to scare people into heaven, consider the above passage and Jude 23 on the place of the fear of the Lord in motivating us to reach the lost.

3)   While the reality of hell underscores God's justice, we must keep in mind other aspects of the nature of our great God. Consider the following passages to describe the character of a God whose heart is broken every time a sinner slips into hell.

a)   He grieves over the wickedness and lostness of man (Genesis 6:5-6 ♦ Judges 10:16 ♦ Psalm 95:10 ♦ Isaiah 53: 3 ♦ Ezekiel 6:9 ♦ Ephesians 4:30)

b)   He is not willing that any be lost (Ezekiel 33:11 ♦ John 3: 16 ♦ 1 Timothy 2:4 ♦ 2 Peter 3:9 ♦ 1 John 2:2)

c) He is slow to anger, full of compassion and mercy (Exodus 34:6-7 ♦ Numbers 14:18 ♦ Psalm 78:38, 86:15, 145:8 ♦ Micah 7:18-19 ♦ Romans 8:37-39, 12:1 ♦ 2 Corinthians 1:3-4)

d) He rejoices in doing good (Deuteronomy 30:9 ♦ Jeremiah 32:41 ♦ Luke 10:21, 15:7 ♦ Acts 10:38)

e) God is love (1 John 4:16)

CHAPTER 14

Motive #4: The Last Days

In the twilight years of his life, Billy Graham has been the subject of many interviews. During one interview on Larry King Live, he was asked what the biggest surprise of his life was. Billy reflected for a moment and replied, "How short it is!" Ask any senior citizen that question, and they will quite likely echo Dr. Graham's observation.

When Rolling Stones leader Mick Jagger first sang, "Time is on My Side," it seemed to him that his wild times would roll on forever. But one look at Jagger today will show you that time is not on his side, or anyone else's for that matter. Our individual lives are incredibly short in light of human history, and they could get shorter because of unfolding world events. There's an increasing awareness among Christians and non-Christians alike that the "End Times" events predicted by Jesus and other Biblical writers are quickly coming upon us. Interest in these "signs of the times" has fueled the amazing popularity of the *Left Behind* series written by Tim LaHaye and Jerry Jenkins.

Before Jesus gave the Great Commission, He spent 40 days instructing His disciples about the kingdom of God and coming world events. I suppose if we had tapes from those sessions, we would have fewer arguments about when Jesus is coming back again! However, the disciples didn't seem to be listening closely because they later asked the resurrected Jesus, "Will You at this time restore the kingdom to Israel?" (Acts 1:6). Their question reflects at least three wrong assumptions. First, they envisioned the overthrow of Rome because they thought the kingdom was political. It is not. It is spiritual. Secondly, they thought the kingdom of God was national—relating exclusively to Israel. It is not. It is international and for the whole world. Thirdly, they thought the kingdom would come immediately. It did not. The kingdom was inaugurated at Pentecost, but it won't reach its fullness until Jesus returns. Because Jesus understands our human tendency of focusing on things that benefit us now, He assured the disciples, through the angels, that He was coming back again physically (see Acts 1:9-11). However, before His ascension, He corrected their focus. He said, "It is not for you to know times or seasons which the Father has put in His own authority. But you shall receive power when the Holy Spirit has come upon you; and you shall be witnesses to Me in Jerusalem, and in all Judea and Samaria, and to the end of the earth" (Acts 1:7-8).

Throughout church history, there have been many views regarding the sequence of events before Jesus returns. But the key question should be: how do our views of the end times affect our passion for reaching the nations with the Gospel? I believe we should proclaim the soon return of Christ simply because it will fuel our urgency to get the job done. A confident expectation that Christ is at the door has always fueled the fires of world evangelization.

Michael Green, one of the foremost authorities on early church history, has said,

> There can be no doubt that the expectation of the imminent return of Christ gave a most powerful impetus to evangelism in the earliest days of the church...the primitive preaching frequently came to its climax in a proclamation of the imminent return of Christ and a challenge to repentance and faith in the light of the culmination of all things. Christians believed they were living in the last days and accordingly redeemed the time by taking every opportunity for evangelism.
>
> It is assumed almost without discussion in contemporary New Testament scholarship that the earliest Christians not only supposed but also taught that the *parousia* (the coming of Christ) and the culmination of all things would be within their lifetime...It is hardly surprising, therefore,

that not only in the First and Second Centuries, but in later periods of the church, missionary zeal has often flowered most notably in circles which held a strongly realistic hope and a likely expectation of the coming Kingdom.[25]

New Testament writers encouraged believers to live with an expectancy of the Lord's soon return. Peter wrote, "And when the Chief Shepherd shall appear, ye shall receive a crown of glory that fades not away" (1 Peter 5:4, KJV). Referring to the same event, Paul wrote, "When Christ, who is our life, shall appear, then shall ye also appear with him in glory" (Colossians 3:4, KJV). To the Philippians, he wrote, "For our citizenship is in heaven; from whence also we look for the Saviour, the Lord Jesus Christ" (Philippians 3:20, KJV). To Titus, "looking for the blessed hope and glorious appearing of our great God and Savior Jesus Christ" (Titus 2:13). And in Hebrews, "Unto them that look for him shall he appear the second time without sin unto salvation" (Hebrews 9: 28, KJV).

A logical question at this point is: why would God put a hope in the imminent coming of Jesus Christ into the hearts of generations throughout church history when He knew He was not going to return in their generation? I believe the answer lies in God's knowledge of the nature of man. God knows that if we live with no concern about Christ's return, we tend to be earthbound and unmoved at the state of the perishing millions around us. He also knows that if we look to a specific time for Christ's return, we tend to be further sidetracked from our primary mission. There have been many fanatics and doomsday prophets who have given specific dates for the coming of the Lord or the end of the world. Obviously, all have been wrong, but these should not turn us off from a positive viewpoint on the Second Coming of Christ. Many significant revivals in church history have been fueled by a strong hope in the coming of the Lord.

A Last Days Outpouring

With this in mind, I would like to talk about a second hope that I believe Jesus wants His disciples to have. As we move from Acts chapter 1 to chapter 2, we see Peter claiming that the Day of Pentecost was a direct fulfillment of a prophecy given in the Book of Joel about God pouring out His Spirit in the last days. Is it possible that there could be a more complete fulfillment of Peter's prophecy in the last of the last days? Notice some of the details in Peter's prophecy: 1) That it would be a worldwide outpouring ("upon all mankind"); 2) That it would be primarily upon young people ("Your sons and your daughters shall prophesy, your young men will see visions..."); 3) It would be an outpouring that would be primarily evangelistic ("And it shall come to pass that whosoever shall call upon the name of the Lord shall be saved"); and 4) It would be multi-generational, involving both genders ("...sons, daughters...young men and women...old men"). One does not have to look very far to see the empirical evidence today of an outpouring of the Holy Spirit in all four of these areas.

Let's take a quick world tour and examine evangelistic growth in the last 100 years. In 1900, there were less than 20,000 evangelical believers in all of Latin America. In the year 2000, there were close to 60 million. In Sub-Saharan Africa, where there were less than 200,000 evangelical believers at the turn of the 20th century, as we enter the 21st century, there are now upwards of 40 million believers (half of the entire population). Seoul, Korea, had no churches in the year 1900. Today, there are over 7,000 churches in Seoul alone, with seven of the ten largest churches in the world residing in that one city. Thirty-five percent of the population of South Korea confesses to be Christian.

Indonesia, the largest Muslim nation in the world, has seen 15 to 20 million people come to Christ since 1965. More Muslims have come to Christ in the last 20 years than in the previous 1,400 years of Muslim evangelism combined. Since 1960, the number of evangelical Christians in Western nations has doubled from 50 million to 100 million. In the developing nations, the Christian growth is *seventeen-fold*—up from 25 million in 1960 to over 425 million today! Worldwide Christian growth has gone from under 5 percent in the year 1900 to over 11 percent today.[26] Regularly, reports come into my office of young people afire for God in many nations of the world. Sons and daughters are prophesying, young men are seeing visions, old men are dreaming dreams, and God is pouring out His Spirit.

Could it be that along with the predicted apostasy that was to happen at the end of time, there would be a parallel outpouring of God's Spirit while things were getting darker and darker (see 2 Thessalonians 2 and Matthew 24)? As the darkness gets darker, is it possible that God would turn on the light brighter and brighter?

Billy Graham has said:

I believe there are two strains in prophetic scripture. One leads us to understand that as we approach the latter days and the Second Coming of Christ, things will become worse and worse. Joel speaks of 'multitudes, multitudes in the Valley of Decision!' The Day of the Lord is near in the Valley of Decision. He is speaking of judgment.

But I believe, as we approach the latter days and the Coming of the Lord, it could also be a time of great revival. We cannot forget the possibility and promise of revival, the refreshing of the latter days of the outpouring of the Spirit promised in Joel 2:28 and repeated in Acts 2:17. That will happen right up until the Advent of the Lord Jesus Christ.

Evil will grow worse, but God will be mightily at work at the same time. I am praying that we will see in the next months and years the 'latter rains,' a rain of blessings, showers falling from heaven upon all the continents before the Coming of the Lord. There is a mystery of iniquity, but there is also a mystery of righteousness and both are working simultaneously.[27]

Many notable evangelical authorities believe there will be an outpouring of God's Spirit in the last days worldwide. Robert Coleman has an excellent book called *The Coming World Revival*. Campus Crusade for Christ founder Bill Bright has written a book called *The Coming Revival*. And Jonathan Edwards, the leader of America's first Great Awakening, prophesied an outpouring of the Spirit worldwide in the last days before the coming of the Lord.

In light of all this, I find myself in kind of a healthy, spiritual schizophrenia. On the one hand, I would echo with John the apostle, "Even so, come Lord Jesus," and have a confident expectation of His coming. At the same time, I am busy promoting the kingdom of God because God wants us to occupy until He comes. I believe He would have us stop arguing about the timing of the Second Coming and agree that we need to reach the 2 billion people who have yet to hear about His First Coming! In any event, the time is short, and we have work to do—let's go!

STUDY GUIDE

CHAPTER 14

1) The main point of chapter 14 is that we should maintain a healthy expectancy for the return of Jesus, which will help fuel our urgency to get the job of world evangelization done. Consider the following benefits to our Christian life such an attitude would bring and thereby make us more effective in our witness for Jesus.

Abiding in Christ – 1 John 2:28
"Blameless" living – 1 Thessalonians 5:23
Good stewardship – Luke 19:13
Joyful expectation – Titus 2:13
Obedience – 1 Timothy 6:14
Personal purity – 1 John 3:1-3
Readiness – Matthew 24:44
The exercise of our spiritual gifts – 1 Corinthians 1:7

2) The following passages speak of the timing of the return of Christ as sudden, unknown, and imminent (i.e. could happen at any time). In light of this, how do these facts ignite your passion to get on with the business of evangelizing the world?

See: **Matthew** 24:27, 36 ◆ **Luke** 12:35-40 ◆ **Acts** 1:11 ◆ **1 Corinthians** 15:51-52 ◆ **Philippians** 4:5 ◆ **Colossians** 3:4 ◆ **1 Thessalonians** 4:15-17, 5:1-2 ◆ **Hebrews** 10:37 ◆ **1 Peter** 5:4 ◆ **2 Peter** 3:10 ◆ **James** 5:8 ◆ **Revelation** 3:11, 22:20

3) Meditate on 2 Timothy 4:1-8 keeping in mind it was the last chapter of Paul's final letter. Notice his urgency as we realize the following facts.

a) As the "last days" progress, "perilous" times will be filled with ungodliness and spiritual deception (2 Timothy 3, 4: 3-9).

b) Jesus is coming again to judge the world and set up His kingdom (2 Timothy 4:1).

c) Therefore we should "preach the word" whether it is "convenient" or not (2 Timothy 4:2).

d) There will be false teaching within (2 Timothy 4:3-4) and "afflictions" from without (v. 5), therefore we should "do the work of an evangelist."

e) All of us have a limited amount of time—we are all going to die (v. 6)—hence all the more urgent to get the Gospel out.

f) There is a reward, a "crown of righteousness," that will be given to us who are faithful to fight the fight and finish the race and who "love His appearing" (vs. 7-8).

CHAPTER 15

Motive #5: Abundant Life

Easter Sunday of 1998 stands out as one of the happiest days of my life. It began with a spectacular sunrise service on the South Shore of Oahu, after which I dunked several people in the Pacific Ocean at a Calvary Chapel baptismal service. Then I took my family to The Original Pancake House for breakfast. Over the din of clanging dishes, nearby conversations, and the restaurant's background music, my wife Linda asked my son Daniel (then 19) to share a personal story with me.

He proceeded to tell me about a troubled young man who came to our ministry searching for answers. In his humble way, Daniel explained how he had befriended this youth and led him to Christ. Even though he was raised as a preacher's kid, this was probably Daniel's first real "convert." He then looked at me across the table through the long, stringy locks of his sun-bleached hair and said, "Dad, I figure, what else is there to life but getting to know God and leading other people to Jesus? I've decided to drop out of junior college and go to Africa to get some training, and after that I want to pursue the ministry. What else is there?"

As I realized that he "got it" (the revelation that really knowing God and making Him known is the essence of life), I began to cry right there over my pancakes! Like he said, "What else is there?"

For years, I had made it a point not to pressure my boys to follow my footsteps into the ministry. As long as they were serving God, it mattered not to me whether they were a bishop, a baker, or a candlestick maker. However, what hit me that Sunday morning was that it was possible for Daniel to pursue things in his life that, while not sinful, were not the highest that God had for him. That morning it was as if a veil had somehow been lifted from Daniel's eyes so he could see God's priority for his life. Paul prayed for the Ephesians that God would give them a "spirit of wisdom and *revelation*" in the knowledge of Christ (see Ephesians 1:17). That revelation refers to a spiritual understanding of the life that Jesus has to give us and wants to transfer through us to others by means of evangelism.

In the Greek language, "zoe" is the word for *life*. The ancient Greeks used it not only to describe a length of days in which the brain is functioning and the heart is beating, but a higher quality of life that can be contrasted with the animal form of mere existence. The poet Henry David Thoreau sadly observed, "The mass of men lead lives of quiet desperation." It doesn't take a rocket scientist to realize that many people are merely *existing* in bodies and souls that were designed by God to experience His zoe—the kind of life God has to offer.

The Greeks believed one could only obtain zoe through years of strict discipline, education, or escape from the material world. But the Bible clearly shows that the abundant life can be obtained simply through a relationship with Him who is life (see John 14:6). In the Gospel of John, we see clearly that Jesus is the source of that new life. Here are some examples:

* "I have come that they may have life, and that they may have it more abundantly" (John 10:10).

* "In Him was life, and the life was the light of men" (John 1: 4).

* "I am the bread of life" (John 6:35).

* He describes Himself as the source of "living water" (see John 4:10).

* He spoke the "words of eternal life" (see John 6:68).

* His words were "spirit and life" (see John 6:63).

I've heard many terms to describe this abundant life, but whether you call it being Spirit-filled, radical for Christ, abandoned to God, in Christ, or on fire for the Lord, it's the most exciting lifestyle imaginable. The people I know who are "full on" for Christ are living advertisements of God's power and grace. They have a confidence that comes from knowing their eternal destiny, a peace that comes from having a clear conscience, a grace in relationships that comes from knowing that they have been forgiven much, and a joyful expectancy about life that comes from knowing God is in control, not them. And that's not all. They have an intimate relationship with their Father God, rich friendships with fellow Christians, abundant provision in times of need, and the faith and courage to overcome difficult circumstances of all kinds. On top of all that, they're never going to die!

In our lifestyle of evangelism, we have the privilege of sharing with people the good news that they too can share in this abundant life. Certainly, we must press home to them the issues of heaven and hell, but they also need to know that Jesus loves them and has a "wonderful plan for their lives."[28] This plan relates to more than just their eternal destiny. It's about bringing the transforming, abundant life of Jesus into hopeless and dead situations right here on the earth.

I can say with great authority that Jesus can transform lives for the present and for eternity because He did it for me. As a young man, I was caught up in a vicious cycle of drugs, alcohol, and incessant partying. I was aimlessly searching for the good life, but it wasn't until I met Jesus Christ that I experienced zoe and found out why I was put on this planet.

Many people today are searching just like I was. Some try to find meaning and purpose through materialism, mysticism, or marriage; others through professional achievement, worldly pursuits, or escapist pleasures. But only Jesus can satisfy our deepest needs. He once said, "For what is a man profited, if he shall gain the whole world, and lose his own soul?" (Matthew 16:26, KJV). In this question, He was contrasting the value of temporal and eternal life. Obviously, His highest priority—and therefore ours—is leading people into an eternal relationship with Him. But Jesus doesn't want us to neglect the physical needs of those we seek to save. He is the same Savior who fed the multitudes, healed the sick, and showed compassion to the broken-hearted.

Amy Carmichael, the great missionary to India, was once chastised by some of her missionary leaders for spending too much time alleviating the temporal suffering of the girls she was working with at her orphanage in Dohnavur, India. Amy, in a kind letter back to her superiors, acknowledged that eternal life was the most important thing, but she proceeded to say, "...One cannot save and then pitchfork souls into heaven ... souls are more or less fastened to bodies ... and as you cannot get the souls out and deal with them separately, you have to take them both together."[29]

Through the centuries, she and other missionaries have discovered that people become more willing to receive our message of eternal salvation after we've first shown compassion for their temporal "felt" needs. General William Booth, of the Salvation Army, once remarked, "Don't ever preach the Gospel to someone with a toothache. First, get their tooth fixed, and then preach the Gospel unto them. No one ever got saved who had a toothache—they're too busy thinking about their tooth to think about eternal life."[30]

Don Stephens, the founder of Mercy Ships, makes the same point in the heart-wrenching story of a young African named Patrick Coker. Because of a grotesque tumor on the side of his face, Patrick was subjected to daily ridicule in his village and painful rejection by his parents. Patrick was not allowed to eat with them or be seen with them, lest he bring shame upon his family or the village. His life was a painful and seemingly hopeless cycle of deprivation and alienation until Mercy Ships' surgeons and staff extended the love of Jesus to him. They were able to excise the tumor from Patrick's face, restore his facial structure through plastic surgery, and impart to him a sense of dignity and hope. "After this, it wasn't very hard for our staff to tell him and his family and his village about a God who cares for them,"[31] said Don. Mercy Ships has four ocean-going vessels that provide free medical and community services to the poor and needy in Latin America, Africa, Asia, and the Pacific. The staff regularly releases testimonies of people coming to Christ as the love and life of Jesus was demonstrated in practical ways.

Although there are no "pat" answers to the difficult and sometimes complicated questions related to human suffering, we know much of it can be alleviated by plugging into a relationship with the God who sent His Son to give us abundant life. The alternative is aligning ourselves with the "thief who comes to steal, kill, and destroy" (see John 10:10). We must therefore go into all the world and challenge others to choose life.

STUDY GUIDE
CHAPTER 15

1) The main point of chapter 15 is that Christ died not only to save us from the penalty of sin, but its power. He came to give us quality of life, not just quantity. Reflect on the following passages on the victorious Christian life, and keep these promises in mind as you share the hope of salvation with the lost.

o Matthew 1:21 – He came to save us from our sins.

o Matthew 6:25-34 – We can be free from worry.

o Matthew 7:7-11 ♦ John 15:7, 16:23-24 ♦ James 5:16 ♦ 1 John 3:22, 5:14-15 – We can have our prayers answered.

o John 3:16 ♦ 1 John 5:13 – We can have the assurance of eternal life.

o Acts 13:38, 26:18 – We can have the assurance of our sins forgiven.

o Romans 8:1-4 – We can "fulfill the righteousness of the law" by walking in the Spirit.

o Romans 8:37 – We are "more than conquerors" through Him.

o 1 Corinthians 15:35-58 – We have been promised a new body.

o 2 Corinthians 2:14 – We have been promised to "always triumph" in Christ.

o Galatians 1:4 – We can be "delivered from this present evil age."

o Galatians 5:1 – We can be "set free" from the "yoke of bondage."

o Ephesians 1-3 – God gives us 41 promises as part of our inheritance in Christ. Count them and rejoice!

o Colossians 1:13 – We have been delivered from the "power of darkness" and "translated" into Christ's kingdom.

o 2 Timothy 3:15-17 – We have been given God's Word – the Scriptures.

o Hebrews 3-4 – We have been given the promise of continual "Sabbath rest."

o 2 Peter 1:3-4 – We have been given "all things that pertain to life and godliness" and "exceedingly great and precious promises" whereby we can partake of the Divine Nature.

The Gospel is Good News!

2) Just before He gave us the parable of the Rich Fool, Jesus said, "…a man's life consisteth not in the abundance of the things which he possesseth" (Luke 12:15, KJV). Reflect on this statement and the parable and contrast the two choices our non-Christian friends have between the "life" our possessions give us and Jesus' abundant life.

3) Consider the following passages on the "social" aspects of the Gospel and reflect on why the good news of Jesus not only relates to the "by and by" but the "here and now!"

a) The example of Jesus:

   i) He fed the hungry - Matthew 14:15-21, 15:32-38 ♦ Mark 6:37-44, 8:1-9 ♦ Luke 9:12-17 ♦ John 6:1-14

   ii) He healed the sick - Matthew 4:23-24, 8:1-3, 9:1-8, 35 ♦ John 5:1-9, 9:1-7

   iii) He cast out demons - Matthew 4:24 ♦ Mark 1:23-27, 3:11 ♦ Luke 4:33-36, 8:29-36, 9:42

   iv) He turned water into wine to serve at the wedding in Cana - John 2

b) The teaching of Jesus:

He told His disciples to feed the hungry, heal the sick, cast out demons, serve and love one another, clothe the naked and visit those in prison - Matthew 10:1-8, 25:31-46 ♦ Mark 3:13-15 ♦ Luke 9:1-2, 10:9 ♦ John 13:14, 34-35

c) The teaching of John the Baptist:

He taught the tax collectors and soldiers to be just in their social dealing with their fellow man - Luke 3:12-14

d) The teaching of the Apostles:

i) The early church shared their possessions - Acts 2:44-47, 4:32-35

ii) The Apostles dealt with social injustice - Acts 6:1-7

iii) Paul, Peter, James, and John all taught social justice and concern for the poor and needy - Galatians 2:10 ♦ Romans 12:13 ♦ Ephesians 4:28 ♦ 1 Peter 3:8, 4:9 ♦ James 2:14-26 ♦ 1 John 3:17-18

SECTION IV

The Methods of Sharing the Good News

And He said, "The kingdom of God is as if a man should scatter seed on the ground, and should sleep by night and rise by day, and the seed should sprout and grow, he himself does not know how. For the earth yields crops by itself: first the blade, then the head, after that the full grain in the head. But when the grain ripens, immediately he puts in the sickle, because the harvest has come."

—Mark 4:26-29

A few years ago, I read an interesting statistic regarding evangelism. The American Institute of Church Growth has calculated that the average convert to Christ in North America has 5.7 evangelistic encounters before he makes a final decision for Christ.[32] As I reflected on my own testimony of how I became a Christian, I was surprised to remember that I had approximately six encounters with the Gospel before I was converted.

I observed that my Roman Catholic upbringing helped keep the ground of my heart soft toward the Gospel. Then the "seed" was planted in me when two guys named Kevin and Kelly approached me on a beach in Santa Cruz, California, and handed me a Gospel tract. I then proceeded to buy a Bible and began reading it, which further watered the seed that had been planted. A friendship with a Christian co-worker in the restaurant where I was working as a dishwasher further watered the seed. A Billy Graham Crusade, *The Ten Commandments*, and even a Led Zeppelin album helped water the seed that was planted in my heart that day on the beach. Finally, six months after I had first heard the Gospel, I was ready to be harvested.

To take our parable a step further, if we interpret the ground being the ground of a person's heart, the seed being the Word of

God (the Gospel), the water being the convicting work of the Holy Spirit upon the Word of God as it is placed in our heart, and the harvesting representing when a person actually receives Christ, we can see that having the proper tool at the proper time is of utmost importance.

The "tools" of evangelism are our methods of sharing the Gospel. Throughout church history, God has used hundreds of methods to bring people to Jesus Christ. That's why I get concerned when people focus exclusively on one method. Every time a new book is written on a different strategy of evangelism, I find myself being a bit uneasy. I'm happy that someone else is equipping the saints to win the lost, but I also cringe when authors make over-statements which reduce evangelism to such a simple formula that the Holy Spirit seems hardly needed. "Just love them in" or "just live the life" are two examples. The fact is each of these statements (and hundreds more) may be true <u>depending</u> on the situation at the given time.

In this section of our study, we will be using Jesus' seed-planting parable as our template to go through five methods of evangelism. We will be looking at plowing the ground, preparing the soil, planting the seed, harvesting the crop, and marketing the produce; all to be done at the proper time and under the Holy Spirit's direction.

THE METHODS

Evangelistic Methods	Biblical Example	Evangelistic Focus	Bottom Line	Relevant Scripture
Pre-evangelism	Paul	Plowing the Ground	Apologetics	(1 Peter 3:15)
Presence-Evangelism	Church in Antioch	Preparing the Soil	Corporate Witnessing	(Acts 1:8)
Proclamation-Evangelism	Philip	Planting the Seed	Individual Witnessing	(Luke 24:47)
Persuasion-Evangelism	Peter	Putting in the Sickle	Soul-winning	(Acts 2:38)
Propagation-Evangelism	Timothy	Producing the Fruit	Discipling	(2 Timothy 2:2)

CHAPTER 16

Pre-Evangelism

Once while in India, I was seeking to explain the Gospel to a devout Hindu. When I told him he needed to be born again, he looked at me with a quizzical stare. Since he spoke relatively good English, I was perplexed over why he didn't "get it." As I kept trying to explain it, I sensed the Holy Spirit speaking in my ear, "Danny, he is a Hindu. He believes in reincarnation. He already believes he has been born again a couple of thousand times. The thought of being 'born again' is not good news for him. Use a different word picture!" I then knelt down on the ground and drew a figure of a road that forked off into two separate branches—a narrow road, which led to eternal life, and a broad road, which led to destruction (see Matthew 7:13-14). Suddenly a light bulb went off in his Hindu mind, and he began to understand the message of Jesus.

Pre-evangelism involves "preparing the ground" for the Gospel. My shortsightedness concerning my Hindu friend was that I didn't recognize the kind of ground in which I was planting my seed. Each seed kept bouncing up as if it was hitting on concrete. Only when I realized why he wasn't getting my illustration could I change my approach and explain it in a way that he could more easily understand and receive.

Paul told the Corinthians, "The god of this age has blinded the minds of unbelievers, so that they cannot see the light of the gospel of the glory of Christ" (2 Corinthians 4:4, NIV). This verse seems to indicate that, without exception, all unbelievers who have not yet believed in Christ have an actual blinding agent (Satan) who is actively confusing their minds. Pre-evangelism deals with the mind because it is our enemy's first line of defense as he seeks to keep the world in darkness. While the mind remains blinded, truth cannot enter the spirit where the "born again" experience takes place. Hence, the need for prayer and the cautious application of God's Word to remove the spiritual "cataracts" from the non-Christian's eyes.

Because we receive our salvation through faith, some think we don't really need to use our mind in the process. But that's not at all true. God wants us to understand the Gospel we proclaim. In Jesus' well-known parable of the soils, the major difference between those seeds which grew and bore fruit and those who didn't was whether or not they *understood* the message (see Matthew 13:8-23). God invites us, in the first chapter of Isaiah, to "reason together with Him." In 1 Peter 3, we are challenged to "always be ready to give a defense to everyone who asks you a reason for the hope that is in you" And Paul said to the Philippians that he was "set for the defense of the gospel" (see Philippians 1:17). These verses indicate that our intellect is an important tool of understanding what we believe and using it in evangelism. Jesus did command us to love God with all our mind (see Matthew 22:37-39).

Apologetics–the Defense of the Gospel

The Greek word that Peter used when he told us to be ready to give an "answer" is *apologia*, from which we get our word apologetics. This word doesn't mean to apologize for the Gospel, but rather to make a rational defense for it. Living as we are in a society in which Biblical absolutes and Judeo-Christian morals are under attack, we cannot afford to maintain a "God said it, I believe it, that settles it, and if you don't, tough on you" attitude with regards to non-Christians. We must take the time to give honest answers to the honest questions of our generation, be willing to listen to the objections that folks have toward the Gospel, and answer them in a humble and truthful way.

There are two basic types of apologetics that we need to become familiar with in order to reach our generation with the Gospel. The first is what has been termed "pre-suppositional" apologetics. This has to do with us discovering what a person believes and why they believe it. We can then draw their belief system to its logical conclusions, showing them the flaws in what they "pre-suppose."

This is often enlightening for a non-believer because many of them have never thoroughly thought through what they believe. We can then contrast their belief system with one that is based on Biblical truth.

Dr. Mark Eastman, a physician who was strongly skeptical of Christianity, was once given an audiotape featuring the teaching of A.E. Wilder-Smith. He said, "I had spent $150,000 on a college education that was bolstering my belief in evolution and it was destroyed with one fifty-cent plastic cassette tape!"[33] This was simply because Dr. Wilder-Smith had challenged Mark's presuppositions regarding the creation/evolution issue, and gave him answers to questions he hadn't even thought to ask.

Sometimes when I'm witnessing to someone about Christ and they tell me their beliefs about God, the world, reality, etc., I simply ask why they believe what they believe. Often they have no better reason than, "I've always believed it." I then impress on them the importance of knowing whether or not their belief system can stand up to the test of reality. For example, many folks in our culture believe that "all roads lead to God" or that "all religions are right." So when someone says that to me, I lead them down the road of their pre-suppositions, and without even arguing, many see the flaws of their belief system. Other times I just say to a person, "Let's suppose that what you're saying is true." Then I ask them to compare their view to the Biblical worldview. This is sometimes enough to convince an honest skeptic that the truth is in Jesus.

There are many excellent books on pre-suppositional apologetics by authors such as Francis Schaeffer, C.S. Lewis, Norman Geisler, and Ravi Zacharias. There are also good books that challenge the theory of evolution and give scientific evidence for the Biblical account of creation (i.e. *Darwin On Trial* by Philip E. Johnson). Other pre-suppositional apologetics examine the bankrupt philosophies of our day, affirming the truth of Proverbs 14:12 that says, "There is a way which seemeth right unto a man, but the end thereof are the ways of death" (KJV).

The second type of defense is called Biblical apologetics. This involves using the Bible to make a case for the Biblical worldview. Some contend that when you quote the Bible to prove the Bible, you are using circular reasoning, and therefore your conclusion is invalid. However, the Bible stands out as the most historically affirmed of all ancient manuscripts. For example, there is ample historical evidence about Jesus and His followers from Jewish and Roman historians of the 1st century. In his book, *The Case for Christ*, journalist and author Lee Strobel compiles some of this evidence, noting that even historical accounts by those hostile to Christianity help affirm many details recorded in the Gospels.[34]

Another argument is also the mountain of manuscript evidence that supports the accuracy of the Bible. Dr. Bruce Metzger, a distinguished Princeton scholar, said they now have identified 5,664 Greek New Testament manuscripts, some dating back to the 1st century. He noted that there are also thousands of other ancient New Testament manuscripts in other languages. There are 8,000 to 10,000 Latin Vulgate manuscripts, plus 8,000 in Ethiopian, Slavic, and Armenian languages. In all, there are about 24,000 manuscripts in existence.[35] The manuscript evidence for the Bible's accuracy is hundreds of times more reliable than that of other ancient writings, such as Caesar's *Gallic Wars* or Homer's *The Iliad* and *The Odyssey*. After reviewing hundreds of ancient manuscripts, scholars Norman Geisler and William Nix concluded, "The New Testament has not only survived in more manuscripts than any other book from antiquity, but it has survived in purer form than any other great book—a form that is 99.5 percent pure."[36]

We must keep in mind, however, that apologetics alone will never draw a person into the kingdom of God. Faith comes by hearing the Word of God, not reasoned arguments (see Romans 10:17). The value of apologetics lies in the fact that with the application of truth, we can strip away the blinders from unbelieving minds, thus opening the way for the Gospel to come in.

I have witnessed and reasoned with some people who have come to see the truth of the Gospel very clearly, but have still failed to respond to it. We must not forget that it is the Holy Spirit alone, not reason, who ultimately convicts a person of sin. Reasoning with a person, however, does break up the ground so that we can have an opportunity to plant the Gospel in soil that will have the most potential to bring forth fruit.

Once while getting ready to go to a Bible study with my friend Alex, two Jehovah's Witness workers showed up at Alex's door. We talked to the two women for a few minutes, and realizing their purpose, I asked Alex if he would mind me staying behind to talk to these women. He went to the Bible study while I spent the next four and a half hours reasoning with these women about their faith while they tried to convince me that theirs was true. Even though it was a pleasant and unheated conversation for most of the time, we nonetheless "argued" about the Jehovah's Witness viewpoint on the Bible as contrasted with historic Christianity. We went back and forth over the Scriptures in the Gospels as to the identity of Jesus. We talked about what it took for someone to actually be saved. Was it just good works or simple faith in Jesus Christ? I tried to crack the foundation of their belief by pointing out the myriads of false prophecies that the Watchtower Bible and Tract Society has foisted upon the public about the coming of Christ and other unfulfilled prophecies by their seers.

Like two heavyweights at the bell of a 15-round fight, we were all pretty worn out by 11:30 that night. All of a sudden, Janet, the older one (and the one responsible for discipling the younger one), stopped, and with a faraway look in her eyes said something I'll never forget. She said, "You're right. It's just like they taught me in my Baptist Sunday School. Jesus is the Son of God, died for our sins, and it's by grace through faith that we're truly saved." I led her in a prayer to commit her life to Jesus Christ, while her younger J. W. disciple looked on in shock and disbelief! That encounter was several years ago, and recently I ran into Janet and found that she was still walking with the Lord.

A lot of plowing had to take place in that encounter to convince her of the truth of the Gospel. Arguing and disputing with people who have wrong ideas about God is sometimes our lot in evangelism. If the Gospel is being attacked, we must defend it. If the truth is being perverted, we must straighten people out. Paul said it was his "custom" (see Acts 17:2). Paul reminded King Agrippa that one of his assignments on earth was "...to open their eyes, in order to turn them from darkness to light, and from the power of Satan to God, that they may receive forgiveness of sins and an inheritance among those who are sanctified by faith in Me" (Acts 26:18).

STUDY GUIDE
CHAPTER 16

1) Apologetics (giving reasons for and defending the faith) are used by Stephen (Acts 6:11-7:53), Paul, and Peter as a form of pre-evangelism. Some scholars even feel the Book of Acts was written as an apologetic to prove to the Romans that in the early church it was the Jews, not the Romans, who provoked the persecution. Consider the following uses of the Greek word *apologia* and see how you can apply it to your own pre-evangelism strategy:

"...hear my *defense* which I make now unto you..." Acts 22: 1, KJV

"...license to *answer* for himself concerning the crime..." Acts 25:16, KJV

"...My *defense* to those who examine me is this..." 1 Corinthians 9:3

"...and in the *defense* and confirmation of the gospel..." Philippians 1:7

"...I am set for the *defence* of the gospel..." Philippians 1:17, KJV

"...at my first *defense* no one stood with me..." 2 Timothy 4: 16

"...be ready always to give an *answer* to every man..." 1 Peter 3:15, KJV

2) Biblical writers used the creation as an apologetic tool to open hearts to the Gospel. Reflect on the following passages and see how the Scriptures point to a Creator God who "speaks" through His creation:

See: **Psalm** 19:1-6 ♦ **Acts** 14:15-17, 17:24-25 ♦ **Romans** 1: 18-20, 10:17-18

Consider how you can use "creation evangelism" as a way to open hearts to the truth of the Gospel.

3) As with most truth in Scripture, there are balancing elements that must be considered to keep from unbiblical extremes. Keeping in mind the above passages regarding the use of apologetics, consider the "bottom line" on all evangelistic strategy—the preaching of the simple Gospel and its power to save—in the following Scriptures:

See: **Romans** 1:16, 10:9-17 ♦ **1 Corinthians** 1:17-29, 2:1-5, 15:1-4 ♦ **Galatians** 3:8-9 ♦ **Ephesians** 6:19-20 ♦ **Philippians** 1:15-18 ♦ **Colossians** 4:3-5 ♦ **Hebrews** 4:12

CHAPTER 17
Presence Evangelism

On a cloudy morning, June 6, 1944, the largest military invasion force in human history approached Normandy, France, in an attempt to seize control of the European continent from Nazi Germany's stranglehold. Though the beaches of Omaha, Juneau, Utah, Gold, and Sword were stained red with the blood of brave American, British, and Canadian military men, they kept pushing forward, and by the end of "D-Day," a beachhead had been established, and for all intents and purposes, the "war to end all wars" was beginning to end. Though subsequent battles were also significant, the D-Day invasion marked the beginning of the end for Hitler and his hordes.

Generals Eisenhower and Montgomery knew that until there was a presence of allied military might on the European continent, the Nazi war machine could not be broken. Likewise, in spiritual warfare terms, unless the presence of God is established in a geographical area by His church, skirmishes can be won here and there, and a few souls nabbed from the enemy, but not much advance of the kingdom of God will take place.

The Apostle Paul recognized this, and his method of evangelism was to establish "beachheads" of God's presence in every city or country to which he went. Church growth experts note that modern evangelism methods have not supplanted this "beachhead" approach. "The most powerful evangelistic tool under the sun is still the planting of new churches."[37] New churches play a vital role as places for the building up of new converts in the faith and later on for releasing them into evangelistic and other forms of vital ministry.

The Model of 'Body Evangelism'
First, let me emphasize that the church is not a building or an organization, but a group of believers who meet together regularly

for prayer, ministry, Bible study, or service. That means a home meeting or workplace Bible study is just as much an expression of "the church" as a formal service in a large building. Obviously, not all expressions of the church have an emphasis on evangelism, but those that do seem to multiply most effectively when they practice what is called "Body Evangelism."

By this, I mean that the church sees itself not only as a structure to shepherd believers, but also as a vital evangelistic agent. It does not merely focus on those gifted in evangelism. It encourages *everyone* in the church to be involved in evangelism. Through their presence in the community and the living presence of Christ within them, these churches are powerful magnets for drawing people into the kingdom.

Conversions produced by body evangelism cannot be measured as quickly or as easily as those of crusade evangelism. However, the American Institute of Church Growth (AICG) suggests that the percentage of "lasting fruit" produced by body evangelism is much higher than that of mass crusades. Body evangelism usually centers on the equipping of church members to be effective representatives of Christ where they work, live, and play. Through teaching and modeling, they learn to share the Gospel by word, deed, and example. Evangelism becomes quite natural to the members of such churches.

Body evangelism can also be a major support to mass crusades, first by bringing people to them, and then by discipling new converts. Both the Billy Graham and Harvest Crusades report that the over 90 percent of the people who come to Christ at their meetings were brought to the crusades by Christian friends, relatives, or neighbors. No doubt, most of these friends are from churches that promote personal evangelism. Such churches usually work diligently to draw new believers into the life of the church. In a Luis Palau Crusade in Rosario, Argentina, body evangelism accounted for a 50 percent retention rate of the new converts. Area churches, which before the crusade were growing at 1.4 percent annually, skyrocketed over 100 percent. Similar results were reported after crusades in Zambia, Burundi, Australia, and the Philippines.

George Barna, in his book, *Evangelism That Works*, investigated some of the most effective evangelistic churches in America and found that they shared a common philosophy of ministry. The following common elements seemed to be obvious.

Effective evangelistic churches believe:

1) Every person is an evangelistic agent.

2) Evangelism is a lifestyle, not a program.

3) Evangelistic success is not defined within the narrow definitions of decisions for Christ or church attendance, but actual incorporation into the life of the church, often revolving around membership in cell groups.

While many of these churches also stage various evangelistic events, they merely supplement the evangelistic efforts of the individual church members. It should also be noted that all of these churches are led by a pastor with a passion for soul winning and discipleship. If your pastor or church has not yet embraced a vision of evangelism, you can help set an example. Body evangelism initiatives are often sparked by people outside of pastoral ministry. For example, in the early 1990s, several churches with a passion for evangelism, many in Latin America, Africa, and Asia decided to experiment with a new approach to soul winning. It involved Christians inviting non-Christians into their homes for a kind of informal discussion about a number of thought-provoking issues. In this non-threatening environment, people began to ask questions about Christ and the Bible, and many opened their hearts to God. To their surprise, these "evangelistic" cell groups were being used by God to draw many into the kingdom and are continuing to multiply at this writing.

Seeing the Gospel

Paul the apostle, quoting Isaiah, said, "Those who were not told about him will *see*, and those who have not heard will understand" (Romans 15:21, NIV, emphasis mine). Jesus said, "Let your light so shine before men, that they may *see* your good works and glorify your Father in heaven" (Matthew 5:16, emphasis mine). Even though words ultimately lead people to Christ (see 1 Corinthians 1:18), words alone are often not enough. People need to *see* a demonstration of the Gospel as well as its explanation. So whether we call it presence evangelism or body evangelism, the church must demonstrate the life of Jesus through active and compassionate involvement in their community. This applies to individual believers as well as the corporate work of the church.

After the massacre at Columbine High School, the government mobilized grief counselors to help the kids who had been traumatized. However, many of the counselors sat in empty offices wondering where all these distraught kids had gone. It turned out that many went where they knew they could find real answers and comfort—to local churches. The pastors and youth pastors in the Littleton area had established a presence for Christ in the area before the shooting and had established credibility for the Gospel. Therefore, when the tragedy happened, the kids knew where they could go for help.

My friend, Mike MacIntosh, who pastors one of San Diego's largest churches, has twice been commended by the city's mayor for the church's work among the poor and for other positive contributions to the community. Many Bible scholars believe the positive influence of Christians in society is the restraining influence mentioned in 2 Thessalonians 2. While the forces of evil are seeking to destroy peoples and nations, the presence of the Holy Spirit-filled church is thwarting their efforts prior to the Second Coming of Christ.

The fullness of the kingdom of God will not come until Jesus returns, but the church here and now must seek to establish Christ's reign in every area of life. We must be a prophetic voice against evil and injustice. The plight of the poor and the murder of the unborn, for example, should be of serious concern to us who represent the King. The educational system needs kingdom teachers and students who can uphold the banner of righteousness and make a stand against humanism. Countries need politicians who will lead the people of God, implementing His principles of justice and righteousness in secular government. The sports' world needs heroes who can point to the King rather than drugs as the source of their strength. The world desperately needs to see Christian marriages and families that are a representation of Christ's love for the church. Our personal holiness, our love for one another, our concern for our neighbors, our commitment to missions, and even our physical lifestyle all reflect the presence of Jesus Christ on earth, which is only a foretaste of His eternal kingdom which is to come.

STUDY GUIDE
CHAPTER 17

1) The main point of chapter 17 is the corporate witness of the church as an evangelistic agent. It is "us", not just "me", that evangelizes the lost and disciples the nations. Study the following passages where the benefits of our witness together are taught.

   a) The church is built by Jesus to provide a structure in which His command to make disciples can be practically obeyed (Matthew 16:18, 28:18-20).

   b) The church provides a practical structure in which believers may be taught the Word of God, thereby contributing to its growth (Acts 2:42-47).

   c) The church provides a venue in which Jesus' command to love one another can be practically lived out, contributing to our evangelistic impact on the world (John 13:34-35).

   d) The church provides a community of believers where interpersonal problems can be solved Biblically, thereby "multiplying the number of disciples" (Acts 6:1-7).

   e) The church provides a practical structure in which the command to "...provoke one another to love and good works, not forsaking the assembling of ourselves together..." (Hebrews 10:24-25) can be obeyed, thereby providing a sense of belonging to those who join its ranks.

   f) The church provides a place where resources can be pooled together for evangelism, missions, and ministry to the poor (Acts 2:44-47, 4:32, 11:27-30 ♦ Romans 15:26 ♦ 1 Corinthians 16:2 ♦ 2 Corinthians 8 & 9).

   g) The church provides a demonstration of Jesus' vision of a "city on a hill," "the light of the world," and the "salt of the earth," thereby impacting the culture around us (Matthew 5:13-14).

h) The church provides the opportunity for us to live out the unity that Jesus prayed we would have which He said would result in the world believing He was sent by the Father. (John 17:21-23; see also John 13:34-35, Acts 6:1-7, and Psalm 133 where God promises to command a "life evermore" blessing where the brethren dwell together in unity.)

i) When the church functions as God intended, providing "teaching, fellowship, breaking bread and prayers," the Lord adds to its numbers (Acts 2:42-47).

j) The church provides a place of discipline to erring members, thereby preserving its purity and strengthening its evangelistic impact on the world (Acts 5:1-11 ♦ 1 Corinthians 5:1-7 ♦ 2 Corinthians 13:2 ♦ 1 Timothy 1:20 ♦ Titus 3:10-11).

2) The primary function of the church, however, is not evangelism, but the building up (edification) of the body of Christ through teaching, fellowship, breaking of bread, and prayer (Acts 2:42). Consider the following passages that either teach and/or demonstrate that a healthy body will grow evangelistically. (In other words, "healthy sheep reproduce themselves" – Pastor Chuck Smith.)

See: **Acts** 2:42-47, 4:1-4, 4:32-35, 5:41-6:7, 11:19-26, 14:21-23, 17:1-4, 18:11, 19:8-10, 20:20-21, 28:30-31 ♦ **1 Corinthians** 14 ♦ **Ephesians** 2:19-22, 4:11-16 ♦ **Colossians** 2:19 ♦ **2 Timothy** 3:15-17 ♦ **Titus** 2:2-8 ♦ **1 Peter** 5:1-3

3) Meditate on Ephesians 4:11-16, breaking it down phrase by phrase, and apply it to a) the local church; and b) the

worldwide church. Consider the various aspects of church life that contribute to the "increase of the body" in church growth.

vs. 11-12 – Church leadership equips the saints for the work of the ministry.

v. 13 – "Till we come to...
  a) The unity of the faith
  b) Knowledge of Christ
  c) Maturity
  d) "Fullness of Christ"

v. 14 – To be kept from...
  a) Immaturity
  b) Instability
  c) "Winds of doctrine"
  d) Craftiness and deception of men

v. 15 – But speaking the truth in love...
  a) To grow up in "all things"
  b) To grow up in Christ

v. 16 – From whom the whole body (He needs every part)...
  a) "Fitly joined together" (working together)
  b) Held together "by every supporting ligament" (NIV) (Unity)
  c) Proper working of every part (everyone functioning in their gifts)
  d) Grows the body
  e) To build up itself in love

CHAPTER 18

Proclamation Evangelism

Dr. Bill Bright of Campus Crusade for Christ has aptly defined evangelism as "the proclaiming of the good news of Jesus Christ in the power of the Holy Spirit and leaving the results up to God."[38] God's job is to convict, convince, and convert. Our job is simply to do what Jesus commanded, "Go into all the world and preach the gospel to every creature" (Mark 16:15).

The word "preach" conjures up images of Sunday morning pulpiteering or crusade-style evangelism, but the Greek word *kerusso* that is translated preach simply means "to proclaim like a herald." A herald in ancient times announced good news that a conquering general was returning from the battle with the spoils of war. Likewise, we've been called by God to proclaim that Christ has won the victory over sin and death and that salvation is available to all.

So when was the last time you preached this good news to someone? If you need courage or instruction on how to do it, listed below are some practical ideas for proclaiming the Gospel in your world. This section is especially for those who are not evangelists by gifting and would probably never have the opportunity to speak in a mass crusade setting.

Preparation for Proclamation

Get Clean

A few years ago, I realized I had developed an attitude of self-righteous, spiritual pride because I was witnessing more often than my other friends in the church. Ironically, even though I was logging many hours in the field, I was seeing less and less fruit. By His grace, God deeply convicted me of my sin, and I took prayer steps of confession and asked forgiveness. Within a few days, I led several people to Jesus including a Hare Krishna devotee and a man whom I intercepted on his way with a loaded gun to kill his wife and her lover. This couple was reconciled shortly thereafter. God was simply showing me what He could do with a heart surrendered to Him.

If we're honest, most of us must admit that we often pray for the power of God without first seeking the purity of God. Even King David fell into this trap. Then he discovered that he couldn't represent God's salvation until he confessed his sin, repented, and asked God for a new start. His heart cry is expressed in Psalm 51: 10-13 (KJV). "Create in me a clean heart, O God, and renew a right spirit within me. Cast me not away from Thy presence and take not Thy Holy Spirit from me. Restore unto me the joy of Thy salvation, and uphold me with Thy free Spirit. *Then will I teach transgressors Thy ways, and sinners shall be converted unto Thee*" [emphasis mine]. God desires to develop Christ-like character *in us* before He ever gives Christ-honoring fruit *to us* in evangelism. The first step to a lifestyle of evangelism is wiping the slate clean with God and asking Him for a new start.

Get Filled

We often overlook the simple fact that we need the Holy Spirit's convicting power to be truly effective in evangelism. Therefore, a key step of preparation is to simply ask God to fill you with His Holy Spirit (see Acts 1:8). The legendary evangelist D.L. Moody was once preaching at a service in Chicago when he noticed that two women in the front were in fervent prayer. They later informed him that they were praying he would receive the power of the Holy Spirit. Not long after this, Moody sensed a hunger for a deeper experience with God. He described his experience this way:

I was crying all the time that God would fill me with His Spirit. Then, one day in New York—oh, what a day—I cannot describe it...God revealed Himself to me and I had such an experience of His love that I had to ask Him to stay His hand. I went to preaching again. The sermons were not different, yet hundreds were converted. I would not now be placed back where I was before that blessed experience if you gave me all the world...[39]

Evangelism is spiritual work and cannot be done effectively in the energy of the flesh. Peter, without the Holy Spirit, was a whimpering coward who denied he ever knew Jesus. After he was filled with the Holy Spirit, he boldly proclaimed Jesus in the face of great opposition and saw thousands converted. To return to Moody, as a young man, he was once told by an older preacher named Henry Varley, "The world has yet to see what God could do through someone completely surrendered to Him." Moody made a choice that night, "I am to be that man."

I periodically teach evangelism classes at "Crossroads" Missionary Training Schools, where folks over 35 years of age come for training. In one class, I made a statement that aroused the obvious ire of one of the older women present. I made a point that younger Christians in general make more effective soul winners and that most people get saved before age 20. Her 65-year-old body made its way quickly up the aisle when class was over. "I'm going to prove your statistics wrong!" she proclaimed. Then she asked me for a packet of my tracts, grabbed a younger classmate, and they headed out the door. The next day I was sitting out under a coconut tree counseling a new believer—her convert from the previous night. She didn't let my statistics overcome her faith. She was simply filled with the Spirit and God showed up!

We need to go out every day believing that God will use us to bring others to Christ. If we don't expect God to use us in evangelism, we'll get just what we expect—nothing! Don't be concerned if you're not a gifted speaker. God can use anyone who is willing. The more dependent you are on His grace and power, the more He can do through you. For God says in His Word, "My strength is made perfect in weakness" (see 2 Corinthians 12:9).

Be Available

Many times, I've heard pastors say, "God is not looking for ability, but availability." And it's true. When Isaiah saw the Lord's glory, he also saw his own weakness and cried out, "I am ruined! For I am a man of unclean lips, and I live among a people of unclean lips" (Isaiah 6:5, NIV). God didn't condemn him for these shortcomings, but instead cleansed his sins and asked about his availability. Isaiah's enthusiastic response was, "Here am I! Send me" (Isaiah 6:8). God has placed each of us in spheres of influence (our families, neighborhoods, workplaces, and communities) that we are uniquely qualified to reach with the Gospel. His question to us is the same as it was to Isaiah: "Who will go for Us?" Are you available to carry Christ's message?

One simple way that I have found to enhance my availability has been the carrying of evangelistic accessories. Every day when I put on my belt, I strap onto it my leather tract pouch. Even though it sometimes gets in my way, hinders my sleep on airplanes, and creates curious looks from people who wonder if it is a cell phone, beeper, or handgun, it still helps remind me of my availability to share the Gospel.

In my pouch, I keep copies of three or four types of Gospel tracts, invitations to evangelistic meetings, a map of how to get to my church with the schedule of services, a New Testament, a small notebook for recording people's names, phone numbers, and follow-up opportunities, and a pen for recording them. When I have opportunities during the day to share the Gospel or to connect with someone socially, I give them a Gospel tract that has my phone number printed on the back. I often give these tracts to waiters (with a generous tip!), to parking lot attendants, and other service personnel as the situation arises. I recognize that tracts are not the be-all and end-all of evangelism, but they do help concisely present the Gospel.

Once while preaching at a church in San Francisco, a woman approached me after the meeting with the following story: "I was walking down Market Street on my way home from work when I noticed a pamphlet lying on the sidewalk. The title interested me. It said 'How San Francisco Got Its Name!' I had often wondered about that, so I reached down, picked it up, and stuffed it in my purse. As I was eating dinner that night, I read it. Turns out it was a Gospel tract about Father Junipero Serra who named San Francisco after his patron saint—St. Francis of Assisi. An invitation to receive Christ was on the back, and I accepted. The address of this church was also stamped on the back, so here I am. I've been attending here for six months."

Practicing Personal Evangelism

The word "practice" may sound like a dirty word to some Christians as it relates to evangelism, but let's face it, each of us needs to develop our ministry of personal evangelism through practice. Even Billy Graham didn't start out preaching to thousands. He began by taking advantage of whatever opportunities God gave him to proclaim the Gospel, first in one-on-one encounters and then with increasingly larger groups. Personal evangelism is you, with all your strengths, weaknesses, idiosyncrasies, fears, and gifts, sharing with someone else how they can have a relationship with the most important person in the universe—Jesus Christ.

Paul's young friend Timothy wasn't an evangelist by gifting, but he was still called to do the work of an evangelist (see 2 Timothy 4:5). I liken the exercising of our evangelistic muscles to the practice of my favorite sport—surfing. If someone asks me to teach them to surf, the best thing I can tell them is to get on a board and try it. I could give them various books on surfing and oceanography or a subscription to *Surfer* magazine, but none of these would help unless they went out and did it. Just as you learn to surf by surfing, you also learn to witness by witnessing.

As a young Christian, I "graduated" from dishwashing to working on an assembly line in a vegetable cannery. Next to me on line four was Norman, a New Ager convinced that all roads lead to God. We had eight hours together daily of mindless hauling of spinach from line four to line five. I used these hours to "experiment" on Norman different kinds of evangelism approaches. I went from "Santa Claus evangelism" (the rewards without the requirements), to "Frankenstein" evangelism (the requirements without the rewards), to everything in between, including some hellfire and brimstone. One day shortly after Norman had asked Janet (one of my new converts on the job) for a date, I decided to butt in. Quoting the verse about being "unequally yoked" (see 2 Corinthians 6:14), I talked Janet into breaking the date since Norman wasn't saved. This of course made Norman as mad as a hornet. He gave me a couple pieces of his mind and stormed out the factory door on that Friday afternoon. By Monday morning, he was soundly saved and has walked with the Lord ever since. Even in my nosy bumbling, God was able to use me. You might not be an expert, neither was I nor am I now. I firmly believe, and have seen many times, that God honors it when we give it our best shot. Theodore Roosevelt once said, "Far better is it to dare mighty things, to win glorious triumphs, even though checkered by failure, than to take rank with those poor spirits who neither enjoy much nor suffer much, because they live in the gray twilight that knows not victory nor defeat."

Each time you tell someone about Jesus, you get a bit more confident and clear in your presentation. The way you do it should fit your own unique personality. There are approximately one half billion born again Christians in the world today, so there are probably one half billion evangelistic methods. Some people like to offer people Gospel tracts like the Four Spiritual Laws, Four Facts of Life, Five Steps to Peace With God, and Six Quantum Leaps to Jesus—whatever! Others prefer to witness through books, tapes, videos, or over the Internet. When evangelism is worked into your lifestyle, then it becomes a natural overflow of what's inside you, not just a pat formula. It is "Christ in you, the hope of glory" (Colossians 1:27).

Interest Doors

Javier was a young Hispanic sailor stationed at Pearl Harbor when I gave him and his buddy a Gospel tract one night. His friend walked into a bar, but Javier seemed anxious to talk. We sat on the curb, and he retold the following story: "I was hungry for God about six months ago. I met some Christians from a 'holiness' church. I attended several of their meetings and was feeling close to God. One day on my way into church, I forgot to take my Walkman earphones out of my ears. One of the brothers asked me what I was listening to. I told him it was my favorite rock band. They then quoted verses about worldliness and told me I couldn't be saved if I listened to the devil's music, so I stopped going to church."

With my eyeballs protruding out of my head, I decided (after I recovered from shock) to pursue his "interest" of rock music. I told him about some Christian rock bands and proceeded to send him some tapes in the mail along with some Gospel literature. Within two weeks, he was converted, and I had the privilege of baptizing him. In my humble opinion, the holiness brothers had missed a stepping-stone opportunity, mistaking it for a stumbling block. Rock 'n' roll was Javier's interest door.

God will bring opportunities to share the Gospel into every believer's life. And of course, we could just wait for those doors to open. However, I believe that our wonderful, creative God wants us to use the gifts and interests He's given us to *create* some evangelistic opportunities. These take the form of what I call "interest doors." An interest door is a common interest that we either have or choose to pursue through which we can share the Gospel. These initiatives should reflect our own unique temperaments and personalities. I've seen many examples: people joining clubs to reach out to others with a common interest; musicians writing songs with a salvation message; folks witnessing through the Internet; older mothers mentoring young single moms; mechanics and other tradesmen helping needy families; artists doing evangelistic puppet shows for kids; business people hosting luncheons; and the list goes on and on. It can be any creative initiative to penetrate non-believer's hearts.

Campus Crusade for Christ, for instance, produces a video every year that Christian sports fans can show their guests at half time of the National Football League's annual Super Bowl.

It features testimonies of Super Bowl athletes who have become Christians, and it's a great way to initiate conversation about Christ with your non-Christian neighbors.

I've seen hundreds won to Christ through the "interest doors" of skateboarders and power lifters who do feats of skill and strength to attract young people. I've seen Christians from indigenous groups use cultural dances and celebrations to open the hearts of many other native peoples. I've even seen former gang members using rap music to penetrate the urban youth culture with the Gospel. The common thread in all these is an intentional effort to find "doors" of common interest for proclaiming the message of Jesus Christ. If you have a heart for proclaiming the Gospel, God will give you creative ways to do it.

Mike Ramsey is a missionary from Corona, California, who previously served as a firefighter. Due to an accident on the job, he was rendered unable to be employed any longer in his occupation. Through a series of events, he answered God's call, along with his family, to reach the city of Iliolo on the Philippine Island of Panay. He began his ministry there, however, by visiting the local Iliolo fire station and befriending the local firefighters. He was able to lead many to Christ. Firefighting was Mike's "interest door." What is yours? Examine your life and see how your interests can be a bridge to those around you who need to know the Lord.

STUDY GUIDE
CHAPTER 18

1) Chapter 18 is really the centerpiece of this book—the simple proclamation of the Gospel of Jesus Christ. Upon reading the New Testament, no one could doubt that, in spite of much opposition, the early disciples were very effective in their evangelism. Consider some of the following reasons:

Top Ten Reasons for Effective Evangelism

a) Their passion for souls came from their passion for God. They were a praying, worshipping people who (even their enemies admitted) "...had been with Jesus" (Acts 4:13). [See also Acts 1:14, 2:47, 4:31, 12:12, 13:2-4.]

b) They preached from the Scriptures (Acts 2:17-21, 25-28, 34-35, 13:16-25, 33-35, 17:2-3, 18:4, 24-26, 19:8-10, 24: 14-15, 26:22-23, 28:26-27).

c) They had been trained "on the job" (Matthew 10 ♦ Luke 9, 10 ♦ Acts 13:1-13, 20:4 ♦ Philippians 4:9 ♦ 2 Timothy 2: 2).

d) They were courageous when facing persecution (Acts 5: 40-41, 9:20, 14:19-21, 16:24-25, 22).

e) They were empowered and directed by the Holy Spirit (Luke 24:49 ♦ Acts 1:8, 2:4, 4:8, 31, 6:3, 8:29, 11:24, 16: 6-7).

f) They preached Christ, not themselves (Acts 2:22-36, 4:12, 8:5, 35 ♦ 2 Corinthians 4:5).

g) They preached locally (Acts 2-7, 11:19-21) and globally (Acts 8, 13-21).

h) They preached "everywhere" (Matthew 10:7-8 ♦ Mark 16: 20 ♦ Acts 8:1, 4, 11:19-21).

i) They discipled their converts (Acts 2:42-47, 15:36, 18: 11, 19:10 ♦ 1 Thessalonians 2:7-12 ♦ Colossians 1:28 ♦ 2 Timothy 2:2) and planted churches (Acts 14:23 ♦ Philippians 1:1 ♦ 1 Thessalonians 1:1 ♦ Revelation 2, 3).

j) They worked together in teams and worked hard to preserve unity* (Mark 6:7 ♦ Luke 10:1 ♦ Acts 6:1-7, 13:1-4, 16:3, 18:1-5, 20:4 ♦ John 13:34-35 ♦ Philippians 1:27-2: 4 ♦ Romans 12:10 ♦ 1 Corinthians 1:10 ♦ Ephesians 4:3, 11 ♦ 1 Thessalonians 3:12 ♦ 1 Peter 1:22, 4:8).

(*See also Acts 15:36-41 – my view is that Paul and Barnabas actually preserved their unity by splitting lest their disagreement over John Mark do further damage to the missionary team.)

2) Romans 10:17 tells us that faith comes by hearing the Word of God. Let your faith for having a lifestyle of effective evangelism "come" by a study of the multitude of Scriptures referring to evangelism and witnessing:

See: **Matthew** 3:1-12, 9:35-38, 10:7-8, 16-20, 11:1, 13:18-23, 19:16-22, 24:14, 28:19-20 ♦ **Mark** 1:14-15, 17, 38-39, 2:2, 14-17, 3:14, 4:14-20, 5:19-20, 6:12, 10:17-22, 13:10, 16:15 ♦ **Luke** 4:18, 5:10, 7:22, 8:1, 9:2, 6, 60, 10:2, 20:1, 24:32, 24: 45-48 ♦ **John** 3:3-21, 4:6-26, 34-38, 18:37, 20:31, 21:24-25 ♦ **Acts** 1:8, 2:14-40, 3:12-26, 4:4, 8-12, 5:20, 28-32, 40-42, 7:2-53, 8:1,4-8, 12, 20-25, 35-37, 9:20, 29, 10:34-43, 11:14, 19-20, 12:24, 13:31-32, 44-49, 14:1-7, 21, 15:7, 35, 16:10, 31, 17:2-3, 16-31, 18:4, 20:20-21, 22:15, 26:16-23, 28:30-31 ♦ **Romans** 1: 16, 10:14-17, 15:16-19, 16:25 ♦ **1 Corinthians** 1:17-23, 2:2-4, 9:14, 16-24, 15:1-4 ♦ **2 Corinthians** 2:12, 4:5, 5:18-21, 10: 14-16, 11:7 ♦ **Galatians** 1:11, 2:2-7, 3:8, 5:11-12 ♦ **Ephesians** 6:18-20 ♦ **Philippians** 2:16 ♦ **Colossians** 1:5, 23-29, 4:3-6 ♦ **1 Thessalonians** 1:5, 2:1-6, 9, 13, 16 ♦ **2 Timothy** 2:24-26, 4:2-

5 ♦ **Hebrews** 2:3-4, 4:2 ♦ **James** 5:20 ♦ **1 Peter** 1:12 ♦ **1 John** 1:2, 5:11-12 ♦ **Revelation** 14:6, 19:9

3) The Bible not only challenges us to witness in our own local setting but in "all the world" (Mark 16:15), "every nation" (Matthew 28:18-19), and to the "uttermost parts of the earth" (Acts 1:8). Study the following passages on God's "eternal purpose" (Ephesians 3:10-11) to fill the earth with "...the knowledge of the glory of the LORD as the waters cover the sea" (Habakkuk 2:14).

See: **Genesis** 12:1-3, 17:5, 16, 18:18, 22:16-18, 26:4-5 ♦ **Exodus** 19:6 ♦ **Numbers** 14:21 ♦ **1 Samuel** 17:46 ♦ **Psalms** 67, 96, 98 ♦ **Isaiah** 44:6, 60:1-3, 61:11, 66:18-19 ♦ **Daniel** 2: 44, 7:13 ♦ **Zechariah** 2:10-11, 9:10, 14:9 ♦ **Matthew** 24:14, 28:18 ♦ **Mark** 13:10, 16:15 ♦ **Luke** 24:47 ♦ **John** 20:21 ♦ **Acts** 1:8, 3:25 ♦ **Romans** 1:5, 15:21, 16:25-26 ♦ **2 Corinthians** 10: 16 ♦ **Galatians** 3:8 ♦ **Colossians** 1:25-27 ♦ **Hebrews** 6:12-18 ♦ **Revelation** 5:9, 7:9

CHAPTER 19

Persuasion Evangelism

A few years ago, I was preaching multiple Sunday morning services at Horizon Christian Fellowship in San Diego while Pastor Mike MacIntosh was out of town. Over 1,500 people were in the first service, so I had high hopes when I concluded my message and gave an invitation for people to receive Christ. To my surprise, there was hardly any response. Since my message was aimed primarily for Christians, I considered whether I should even give an invitation at the second service. When the time came to do so, I was faced with a split-second decision. As the congregation bowed their heads, I paused for a moment and immediately sensed that God wanted me to "go for it." Over 25 people gave their lives to Jesus Christ in response to that invitation.

Two weeks later, I received a note in the mail from a friend of Sean Rohleder. Sean was a university student who had been in San Diego that weekend visiting his girlfriend, a recent convert to Christ at Horizon. She had brought Sean to the second service that morning, and he was one of those who came forward to receive Jesus. After rejoicing with his friends that afternoon over lunch, Sean was driving home to central California and was killed in a car accident on Highway 101. The note from Sean's friend thanked me for being obedient to God and challenging him to give his life to Christ. The time for the harvest had come.

Persuasion evangelism refers to the point in an evangelistic situation where we actually challenge a person to give their life to the Lord. On the Day of Pentecost, after Peter explained the Gospel, his hearers responded saying, "What shall we do?" Peter then put in his sickle and said, "Repent and be baptized, and you shall receive the gift of the Holy Spirit" (see Acts 2:37-38).

Remember the parable of the growing seed and its pictures of the blade, the ear, and the full corn in the ear. There is a time and a place for us to aggressively get out our sickle and persuade people to come to Jesus Christ. I've tried to make it clear in my presentation so far that evangelism or witnessing is not defined in terms of results, but in terms of obedience to Christ's command to go into all the world and preach the Gospel. We must never forget, however, that the goal of all evangelism is the actual winning of people to Christ and making them into disciples. While trying not to be overly pushy, we should nonetheless be aggressive. People's souls are at stake. We should not be indifferent over whether or not people receive Christ, but present it as an absolute necessity.

My friend Lonnie Frisbee was one of the boldest and most perceptive witnesses I've ever seen in situations where he knew it was time to use persuasion evangelism. At Lonnie's funeral a few years ago, Pastor Chuck Smith told a story about a time when he and Lonnie were driving down a street and came upon a horrible accident. Lonnie jumped out and ran over to one of the victims who was lying in a pool of blood, with a fractured skull and lacerations on many parts of his body. Other folks were stroking his hair, comforting him, and telling him everything was going to be all right. Not Lonnie. He looked him straight in the eye and said, "Everything is not all right, you're dying. Do you know Jesus Christ? Do you have the assurance that if you died right now, you would go to heaven?" The young man looked up and said, "No." Lonnie led him to Christ right there on the street. By the grace and power of God, that man recovered from his injuries and became a faithful member of Calvary Chapel. There is a time to sow, but there's also a time to reap!

Charles Finney, in his book *Revival Lectures*, has a chapter called "How to Win Souls." In it he warns of the danger of speaking in general terms when talking to a specific person. He speaks of the necessity of looking people right in the eye, talking in the first person, and telling them frankly that they need to repent and give their lives to Christ.

Persuasion evangelism necessitates a more passionate effort to win people to Christ. This is the time to let them know the seriousness of the issues involved and the importance of making a decision to give their life to Christ. We must be careful, however, not to use emotional manipulation to do so. When the Holy Spirit gives you assurance that the time is right to speak boldly, He will do the convicting. The courtroom illustration I used earlier is an apt picture of the verdict that we want the non-Christian to make concerning Jesus. The testimonies are in, the evidence has been presented, and now it's time for a decision.

Sweet Rewards of Patience

In our American fast-food mentality, we often want to get souls saved in the first five minutes of a conversation. However, as was pointed out earlier, conversion is a process, and it seldom happens instantaneously. If we wield our sickle too early and harvest a premature crop, it's unlikely that we'll get lasting fruit from our effort. I firmly believe that if you ask God, He will give you a sign that the person you've approached is at a decision-point of accepting Christ.

I've done informal surveys in missionary training classes and church services worldwide in which I've asked, "How many of you became a Christian the first time you heard the Gospel?" I have never had more than ten percent of an audience raise their hands. The vast majority indicate that it was a process of God drawing them to Himself, "First the blade, then the ear, after that the full corn in the ear..." (see Mark 4:26-29, KJV).

The point of this is that we should never give up on someone. If we're patient enough, the message will get through somehow. I once became very frustrated in my efforts to reach out to an elderly Japanese-American neighbor named George. Despite my numerous overtures of friendship, George refused to speak to me because I wouldn't take his side in a dispute and remained neutral with another neighbor. Then within a period of about six months, the other neighbor died and George himself was diagnosed with inoperable cancer. As his health failed, a dear Christian lady named Betty began visiting George and his family. She brought meals, comforted them, and showed much kindness. Though they were all devoted Buddhists, Betty also shared the love of Jesus with them. In time, her efforts opened up a door for me to meet with George too.

Betty and I visited him every two days while he was on his deathbed, and each time we encouraged him to confess his sin and give his life to Christ. Each time he said he just "could not believe." But then one day, he asked my forgiveness for snubbing me so long. When he released forgiveness to me, something opened up in his spirit. A few days later, Betty was able to get out her sickle, look him in the eye, and say, "George, you know you're dying. You're about to face eternity. Jesus died for your sins. You must accept Him and turn from your sins now to have the assurance of going to heaven." George not only received Jesus into his life three days before he died, but he asked to have a Christian funeral and asked me to preach the Gospel. Over a hundred of his Buddhist friends showed up, and I was given the glorious opportunity to tell George's story and to give the good news that he was now in heaven, free from his cancer-wracked body, forever to be in the presence of the Lord. Betty had the wisdom (and the boldness) to be persuasive when she needed to be.

The Sinner's Prayer

When a person is ready to receive Christ, you can lead them in a simple sinner's prayer. It goes something like this: "Lord Jesus, I believe in You that You died for me and rose from the dead. I choose now to turn from my sins, and I ask You to come live in my heart. Please forgive my sins, and help me to live a new life in You." Reciting such a prayer is not absolutely necessary for a person's salvation for the Bible says that we are saved when we put our faith in Jesus (see Acts 16:31). However, the evidence of faith is a turning from sin and a willingness to identify with Christ through public confession and baptism (see Acts 2:38 and Romans

10:9). Our job in persuasion evangelism is to secure their decision for Christ and to make sure they understand what they need to do in order to be saved. Once again, I caution you to let the Holy Spirit guide you in the "reaping" process. They can confess Christ, but if there's not a sincere faith, then nothing will change.

Within two weeks after I became a Christian, I read a book by Hal Lindsey called *The Late Great Planet Earth*. It was full of references to the Antichrist, horrific judgments on the Earth, and the return of Christ. I had never heard such things before, and it fired me up with an urgency to win people to Christ before it was too late.

Clad in my tank top and board shorts, I drove over to my best friend Dave's house and persuaded him to go with me to the beach. Dave was wondering what the excitement was all about when I started peppering him with questions: "Did you know that Jesus could come back at any time?" Dave: "I've heard that somewhere before." "Did you know that a great tribulation is coming?" Dave: "No, I never heard that." "Did you know that a man called the Antichrist is going to rise up out of the sea, and if you haven't accepted Jesus, inscribe the number 666 on your forehead which will leave you without hope?" With terror in his eyes, Dave said, "No, I've never heard that before." By instilling fear, I manipulated him into saying a sinner's prayer and then "baptized" him in the ocean. In my infantile Christian understanding, I actually thought I had led him to Christ. In reality, all I had done was get a sinner wet! Eight years later, Dave actually gave his life to Christ during one of my Bible studies (when I was teaching on prayer, of all things!) and is a vibrant Christian today. Because I was ahead of God's timing, I may very well have *retarded* Dave's spiritual growth.

The parable of the growing seed indicates to us that there is timing involved in the different procedures that a farmer uses in order to bring in his crops to yield the greatest harvest. The same is true in the spiritual realm. There is a time for plowing, a time for planting, a time for watering, and a time for reaping. Solomon agreed with this concept when he said, "To everything there is a season, a time for every purpose under heaven" (Ecclesiastes 3:1).

I like to give the following illustration: when I get up in the morning, I put on an invisible evangelism belt. On my belt, I have a seed bag, a water can, a trowel, and a sickle. The trowel is kind of a digging device to prepare the ground of a person's heart in order to receive the Gospel. This is what we referred to earlier as pre-evangelism. The seed bag is for the initial planting of the seed of the Gospel in a person's heart who's never heard it before. The water can is to water seeds that other workers have planted in order to cooperate with God in His process of drawing people to Himself (see John 6:44). The sickle is, of course, the tool that we use in persuasion evangelism.

I find it interesting that in His evangelism parable, Jesus did not say, "Pray to the Lord of the harvest that He would send forth reapers" into His harvest. He did not say, "Pray to the Lord of the harvest to send forth sowers" to His harvest, etc. He simply said, "Pray to the Lord of the harvest to send forth workers into His harvest field." A worker is one who works. He or she does whatever work is necessary to bring in the harvest, and that depends on the timing. When the timing is right, however, we must put in our sickle and reap a harvest of souls for His glory.

STUDY GUIDE
CHAPTER 19

1) The Greek word for "faith" is *pistis*, which means "to be persuaded." The word for "persuade" is *peitho* and is closely related. Realizing God doesn't want us to be overly pushy or manipulative in winning people to Christ, He nonetheless wants us to be "persuasive." Consider the following passages where peitho is used as a part of evangelistic strategy:

See: **Luke** 16:31 ♦ **Acts** 13:43, 18:4, 19:8, 26, 26:26-28, 28:23 ♦ **Romans** 2:8 ♦ **2 Corinthians** 5:11 ♦ **Galatians** 1:10

2) While it can be argued that there is not a "sinner's prayer" in the Bible (the publican comes close, Luke 18:13), there is nonetheless a need for a person to make a clear-cut decision for Christ. Consider the following Scriptures in light of the need for some type of "action" to demonstrate this new faith in the heart of a convert.

a) If we believe, we must "receive" (John 1:12).

b) Jesus said we must choose for or against Him (Matthew 12:30 ♦ Luke 11:23).

c) While baptism is not a condition of salvation, it was nonetheless urged upon believers either immediately or shortly after their conversion (Acts 2:38-41, 8:12, 16, 36-38, 9:18, 10:47-48, 16:15, 33, 18:8, 19:5, 22:16).

d) In Ephesus those who believed staged a public burning of their occultic scrolls. They had been "persuaded" by Paul's preaching, teaching, "special miracles," and the incident with the sons of Sceva (see Acts 19:8-20).

3) Study the following Scriptures and notice that the witnesses for Christ, while relying on the power of the Holy Spirit, nonetheless employed Spirit-led tools of persuasion to arrest the attention of their hearers:

a) Peter "lifted up his voice" at Pentecost (Acts 2:14).

b) They used Scripture to persuade Jews and God-fearers (Acts 2:17-21, 25-28, 34-35, 7:2-50, 13:16-25, 35, 17:2-3, 18:4, 24-26, 19:8-10, 24:14-15, 26:22-23, 28:26-27).

c) While not relying on enticing words of man's wisdom (1 Corinthians 2:4-5), they nonetheless "spoke so effectively" that a great number of Jews and Gentiles believed (Acts 14:1, NIV).

d) They spoke with "boldness" (Acts 4:13, 29, 31, 9:27-29, 13:46, 14:3, 18:26, 19:8 ♦ Ephesians 6:19-20).

e) They used "body language" to communicate. Paul "motioned with his hand" (Acts 13:16, 21:40, 26:1).

CHAPTER 20

Propagation Evangelism

Go therefore and make disciples of all the nations...
teaching them to observe all things that I have commanded
you.

—Matthew 28:19-20

After God first called me to be involved in evangelism, I sometimes
dreamed about how He was going to use me to evangelize the
world. With an inflated ego, I saw myself giving the altar call in
a huge stadium, calling thousands to come forward and accept
Christ. Back then I thought that if we could just hold enough
large rallies, have enough TV and radio exposure, and distribute
enough literature, that the world would be evangelized in no time.
But I discovered that my early ideas about mass evangelism were
both impractical and shortsighted. While mass evangelism has an
important role in extending the kingdom, I was leaving out Jesus'
ultimate model for reaching the world—discipleship.

We evangelists have been notorious throughout church history
for creating a dangerous separation between evangelism and
discipleship. We like to publish newsletters with glowing statistics
of souls saved, hands raised, or other tallies of new converts.
But if we take an honest look at those figures, we must ask how
many continue on in the faith. Biblically, converts were not
counted until they had been baptized and incorporated into a local
church. Estimates from mass evangelism efforts show an average
retention rate of only about 20 percent or less. That shows that we
are not working hard enough to bring together both evangelism
and discipleship. Evangelism without discipleship is not true
evangelism simply because Jesus gave the evangelistic command
to "make disciples." Likewise, discipleship without evangelism
is not true discipleship because the command to make disciples

was given with the evangelistic thrust of the Great Commission in mind.

Billy Graham himself is quoted as saying, "The most important phase in an evangelistic campaign is the follow-up." This is because the object of the Great Commission is not merely to make converts, but rather to see these converts become faithful members of the local church. We can see from the way Jesus trained His disciples and the strategy Paul had for church planting that God is not satisfied with seeing souls saved—He wants these souls to become spiritually mature disciples who can then disciple others.

Producing Fruit that Remains

In the 1960s, evangelist Kenneth Strachen incorporated a new program throughout 11 nations of Latin America called "Evangelism In-Depth." It was highly organized, bathed in prayer, blitzed by the media, supported by high-profile Jesus parades, and complimented by special campaigns for women and indigenous peoples. It was a yearlong program with a vision to equip every member in the church for successful evangelism.

At first, the Evangelism In-Depth campaign seemed quite successful. But a ruthlessly honest evaluation found that church growth, both during and after the campaign, had actually <u>declined</u>. The reason was obvious. As well meaning as this concept is, "saturation evangelism" programs of this type put enormous pressures on participants. They take people out of their normal environments and place them into high-energy evangelistic situations that require large commitments of time, energy, and finances. By the time the one-year program was over, people had to double-up their workloads to catch up on finances and work that had fallen behind during the campaign.[40]

The researchers' most shocking discovery was that the seven denominations that participated in Evangelism In-Depth would have grown much larger if they had NOT done the campaign. They projected that church growth would have increased simply because of the limited amount of "lifestyle" evangelism that was already taking place!

My point in quoting this example and the retention statistics is not to criticize mass evangelism or saturation evangelism. However, I believe that we who are involved in evangelism must be most concerned with long-term results. Jesus said, "I chose you and appointed you that you should go and bear fruit, and that your fruit should remain" (John 15:16). God is not impressed with our evangelistic scoreboard. He is concerned that the people who come to Christ actually become His disciples.

In his classic book, *The Master Plan of Evangelism*, author Robert Coleman points out that in the course of Jesus' three and a half years of ministry, He spent increasingly more time training the twelve disciples and decreasingly less time ministering to the multitudes. While not totally neglecting the masses, He was far more concerned with His long-range objective of making disciples. To quote Coleman: "You cannot outwit the powers of darkness without strict adherence to Him alone Who knows the strategy for victory...only the Master's plan will work..."[41]

The Timothy Principle

Paul's challenge to Timothy was to gather faithful disciples who could learn from him and in turn train other faithful disciples. He says in 2 Timothy 2:2, "And the things that you have heard from me among many witnesses, commit these to faithful men who will be able to teach others also." The key word in this process is "faithful." God wants faithful (reliable) disciples who will stick to His strategy for victory—to win people for Christ, to make faithful disciples of these new believers, and then to send them out to reproduce for the kingdom of God.

When our goal is disciple-making, not decision-making, it helps us in our pre-conversion strategy when seeking to lead someone to Christ. Even before they get saved, we can begin spending time befriending them and spoon-feeding them as much truth as they are able to handle until they are ready to make a decision for Christ. After the decision is made, we simply continue on in a seamless discipleship process of teaching them to obey all of Jesus' commands.

I led a man named Bob to Jesus. At a local hospital, Bob had been diagnosed as a paranoid schizophrenic. After his conversion, he still had problems. We ate together, went to meetings together, and simply hung out. After about six months, I received a call from his probation officer informing me of his progress out of his condition. She further explained that he had been cared for by four separate court-appointed psychiatrists, and I was the only one who had made any significant progress. When she asked what kind of "therapy" I was using, I replied, "Bible reading, studying and memorization, daily prayer, regular church attendance, and helping other people." Clearly unimpressed with my "religious" jargon, she informed me that the judge had cleared it for me to become his fifth court-appointed psychiatrist as long as I agreed to meet with him once a week and hang out! I enthusiastically consented and rejoiced with my wife as I hung up the phone. "Isn't that just like the Lord—to take an ex-acid head who barely made it through high school and make him a shrink for someone who has mental problems when all we are doing is going to church together? Praise the Lord!" Reminds me of a Bible verse: "…when they…realized that they were unschooled, ordinary men, they were astonished and they took note that these men had been with Jesus" (Acts 4:13, NIV). Bob went on to be baptized, married a beautiful Christian lady, and today is a powerful witness for Christ.

So how do we make a disciple? The answer is given to us in the above passage. First, we must *go* to the person (again using our beautiful feet). Then we must seek to lead them to faith in Christ and seal it with baptism. What follows is sometimes a long and painstaking process in which the new believer is taught to follow and obey Jesus in every area of his or her life. We must be prepared to take time to answer their questions, teach them from the Scriptures, and help establish them in a local church. We must become the new disciple's friend and be willing to spend time with them, just "hanging out" with them. Jesus "...appointed twelve, that they might be _with_ Him" (Mark 3:14, emphasis mine).

In disciple-making, Jesus told us to teach them to obey all His commands, and that includes His last commandment—to go and make disciples. An important advantage in the Timothy Principle for the multiplication of disciples is that it is so *do-able*. Most Christians are not ever going to minister to large crowds, but all of us can believe God for one person to make into a disciple. I challenge you to ask God today for a Timothy. Win him, train him, and send him back into the world to do the same for someone else.

Consider this simple comparison of addition with multiplication: if a mass evangelist was to win 1,000 people to Christ every day (with no days off) for the next 30 years (and for the sake of our illustration, none of them fell away), he would win over 10 million people to Jesus. Conversely, if you led one person to Christ this year, then trained that person to win someone else to Christ and to disciple them in the 2nd year (while you also made a disciple in the 2nd year), and if this continued to multiply, within 23 years, you will have gathered over 10 million people into the kingdom of God, all of which are multiplying disciples themselves. If this was to continue on unbroken, by the 35th year, every person on the planet will have become a disciple of Jesus Christ!

I used to think the greatest thrill a person could have, besides actually getting saved, was winning someone to Christ. I have since discovered that an ever-greater joy is seeing someone I have led to Christ leading other people to Christ. It has been a thrill for me many times over to become a spiritual "grandfather." It helps me to realize that the multiplication process is going on and that I'm on the way to my first ten million!

One thing that has helped my wife and me facilitate discipleship is living "in community." Since the early 80s, we have often lived and worked in close proximity to other Christians. For over 20 years, we lived in a small home on the Youth With A Mission (YWAM) base in Honolulu (a camp-like atmosphere for training and sending out missionaries). This kind of setting provides a nurturing environment where spiritual growth occurs quite naturally. It's the closest model I have found to the way Jesus did it.

Paul the apostle also lived among people he was discipling. He must have been thrilled to learn later that his spiritual offspring, the Thessalonians, "became examples to all in Macedonia and Achaia who believe. For from you the word of the Lord has sounded forth, not only in Macedonia and Achaia, but also in every place" (1 Thessalonians 1:7-8).

Throughout church history, those leaders who put an emphasis on making disciples have had the greatest lasting impact. John Wesley, for instance, organized his converts into small groups where "the beginnings of faith in a man's heart could be incubated into saving faith in the warm Christian atmosphere of the society, rather than in the chill of the world."[42] The result of his emphasis on discipleship was one of the most powerful evangelistic and missionary movements in church history—the Methodist Church. It is said that Wesley would "refuse to preach in any place where he could not follow it up by an organized society with adequate leadership." His biographer, Howard Snyder, said, "He was out to make disciples—disciples who would renew the whole church."[43]

A few years ago, I led a three-month outreach to the Fiji Islands. Our strategy was to work with local churches reaching ethnic Indians (mostly Hindu and Muslim) and Native Fijians. During the first six weeks of the outreach, we led over 20 people to Christ and were enthusiastic about winning more. A local pastor, for some unexplained reason, revoked his sponsorship of our team, which, for the next six weeks, rendered it illegal for us to do any religious work.

As we prayed, we felt we were to submit to the immigration authorities and spend the rest of the time discipling the converts we had made, following up on previous contacts, and doing friendship evangelism. Our circumstances squeezed us into placing discipleship on an equal plane with evangelism, where it belongs. The result: 39 baptized converts joined local churches and began growing in their faith. Five went on to become missionaries, and one man (an alcoholic when we met him) became a professor at the Fiji Institute of Technology and today leads the campus ministry there. There are few things sweeter than fruit that remains.

The Scripture tells us that someday the knowledge of the glory of the Lord will cover the earth as the waters cover the sea (see Habakkuk 2:14). How is this to happen? It will happen when we and those we disciple glorify God by our faith and obedience, honoring Jesus Christ in every area of our lives. Then we will be disciples worthy to be called by His name.

So Go For It!

Jesus said, "I came to send fire on the earth, and how I wish it were already kindled!" (Luke 12:49). Evangelistic zeal is like a fire and needs to be fed and stoked continually to keep it burning hot. Human nature tends toward coldness and indifference to spiritual things, especially Gospel work when it becomes uncomfortable. So here are some ideas for how to stoke a passion for personal evangelism:

1) Reread this book and study the Scripture passages cited. Then ask God to give you a consuming desire to see the Great Commission completed.

2) Seek out and get to know other brothers and sisters who are single-minded about missions and revival and who can be examples for you of the lifestyle of evangelism. Let their passion rub off on you.

3) Read biographies of people God has used greatly in evangelism. Talk about revival, evangelism, and missions with

your Christian friends so that you may encourage one another to love and to good works (see Hebrews 10:24).

4) Share with your friends those books, tapes, and CDs that have moved you to a deeper commitment to God and to His purposes in evangelism.

5) Above all, however, begin to witness where you are, remembering that you learn to witness by witnessing. It may be hard at first, but allow God the time to start a fire in you, a fire that will spread to those around you.

Most importantly, get close to Jesus. As we draw close to Him, His desires become our desires and His plans our plans. Spend days in sweet communion with Him, talking to Him as you would to your best friend (He is!). If you abide in Jesus, He has promised that you will bring forth fruit—fruit that will remain (see John 15: 16).

When the Lord returns, may He see the joy of our beautiful feet, busily scampering about the earth, seeking to bring people to Jesus. God loves it when we go.

STUDY GUIDE
CHAPTER 20

1) The main point of chapter 20 is that we must keep in mind that Jesus commanded us to "make disciples," not just "decisions." It is self-evident that multiplication and thereby reproduction is superior to simply the addition of converts. Do a study of the four Gospels and discover Jesus' predetermined strategy to, while not neglecting the multitudes (He fed the 5,000, 4,000, etc.), primarily concentrate on a few. He knew that they, if properly trained, could reach the masses.

2) Keeping the above principle in mind, do a study of Paul's missionary journeys (Acts 13-21, 27-28) and notice Paul's balance of evangelism and discipling. Notice how he:

   a) Follows Jesus' example in his personal discipling of leaders (Acts 16:3, 18:2-4, 20:4).
   b) Plants churches and ordains elders (Acts 14:21-23, 20:17-35).
   c) Follows up with discipleship where he had previously evangelized (Acts 14:21-23, 15:36, 40, 16:1, 18:11, 19:10).

3) Study Acts 16:1-10 compared with Acts 19:9-10. A lesson can be learned not only in divine guidance, but in evangelistic strategy. Paul was forbidden by the Holy Spirit to evangelize Asia and was called supernaturally to Europe. A few years later, however (in God's timing and following His leading), "...all they which dwelt in Asia heard the word of the Lord Jesus, both Jews and Greeks" (Acts 19:10) because Paul ran a dicipleship school in Ephesus.

From this we see the pattern established by Jesus (train the few to reach the many), followed by the apostles in Jerusalem (Acts 2:42-47, 6:4-7), and later taught in Paul's final letter to Timothy. "And the things that thou hast heard of me among many witnesses, the same commit thou to faithful men, who shall be able to teach others also" (2 Timothy 2:2, KJV).

APPENDIX I

The Top Ten Questions Non-Christians
Ask About the Gospel

1) How do we know that God exists?

This question is the bottom line of all spiritual reality. For the non-Christian, if God does not exist, all other questions are irrelevant. At this point, even questions about the Bible being the Word of God or the identity of Jesus Christ are secondary, because if a person does not believe in God, they most likely will not accept the Bible. We must be careful, however, not to engage in what the non-Christian would see as "circular reasoning" (that is quoting the Bible to prove the Bible). There is plenty of objective evidence outside of the Bible for the existence of God, so start with that.

First is the evidence of creation. The Scripture tells us that "...the heavens declare the glory of God" (Psalms 19:1), and the Book of Romans tells us that the created order is visible to all which leaves everyone "without excuse" for their unbelief (Romans 1:20). It is interesting that in the only two instances in the Book of Acts where Paul was dealing with a purely "pagan" (non-Jewish) audience, he opened his sermons by referring to creation (Acts 14 & 17). Even if the non-Christian believes in evolution, he must be pressed to the conclusion that something must have sparked the evolutionary process. The evidence of an ordered universe including the tides, sunrises, sunsets, and seasons of the year all speak of a designed universe—hence a Designer. Logic dictates that we follow the ordered universe back until we come to an "uncaused cause" or an "unmoved mover."

Another evidence for God's existence is that we're all born with a conscience, even those born in places where people have never heard the Gospel. There is an internal witness within us of a basic knowledge of right and wrong. The conscience, of course, can be perverted from God's original intention, but it is nonetheless something all human beings possess. The evidence of creation is our external witness, while the reality of our conscience is the internal evidence that God exists.

A simple visual aid to use at this point would be to quote the "circle of knowledge" illustration. Simply draw a large circle on a piece of paper and make a tiny dot somewhere within the circle. Explain that the complete area within the circle represents all of the knowledge that is in the world, while the dot represents the knowledge that they possess. Then simply ask them if it is possible for God to exist outside of the knowledge they have. Most thinking people with a milligram of humility will acknowledge that this is possible. This might possibly compel a non-Christian friend into admitting that he is agnostic (by definition, someone who doesn't know if God exists) rather than an atheist (by definition, someone who knows that God does not exist). These simple truths will hopefully open them up to further evidence about the existence of God.

2) How do we know the Bible is true?

First, there were hundreds of prophetic predictions given to us in the Old Testament that were fulfilled during the time of Christ. These were given by Hebrew prophets hundreds of years before Christ. Jesus fulfilled over 300 prophecies regarding Himself, many of which could not have been fulfilled simply because He knew they existed. For instance, being born in Bethlehem, being crucified between two thieves, and being buried in a rich man's tomb could not have been self-fulfilling prophecies for Jesus. Other prophecies have been fulfilled since the time the Bible was written, including ones that Jesus gave about the rebirth of the nation of Israel and the return of Jerusalem to Jewish control.

Archeological findings are a second powerful illustration. Every year, more evidence is discovered that confirms that the Bible is the Word of God. For instance, the recent discovery of the Hittite civilization has confirmed Biblical stories. Earlier in the century the discovery of the ruins of Jericho with its walls "falling down flat" just as the Bible says they did gives further evidence to the truth of Scripture.

Another convincing piece of evidence of the Bible's truth is the fact that it still exists. Someone has said that truly "the Bible is an anvil that has worn out many hammers." Many kings, emperors, and despots have tried to destroy the Bible (sometimes literally by burning thousands of copies of manuscripts). It remains with us to this day, and it continues every year to be the world's number one best-selling book. Then there is the evidence of millions of changed lives including the millions of people who have given themselves as martyrs for the cause of Christ throughout the centuries. There is also the moral influence of the Bible throughout the world even in non-Christian lands. Many people who do not profess to have a Biblical worldview will nonetheless complain of human rights' abuses that find their basis in God's Word. If the Bible is not our standard for right and wrong, then we have no basis to complain about human rights' abuses. The Bible ascribes to us our value and therefore our "rights" not to be abused!

Another simple question to ask someone who objects to the validity of the Bible is simply to ask them if they think this world would be a better place if everyone merely followed the Ten Commandments. Just the simple common sense instructions in the Bible about loving one another, respecting one another's values, and serving God and our fellow man should make good common sense to anyone who is willing to think.

3) **Don't all roads lead to God? (What about all of the other religions?)**

This is a difficult pill to swallow, especially for those from countries where religious views have been entrenched for centuries. How could 1 billion Muslims, 300 million Buddhists, and 800 million Hindus be mistaken about their views of God? Hard to swallow or not, the particular truth that there is only one way to God stands as not only evident, but necessary.

As was pointed out earlier in this book, truth is by nature absolute, and most people prove it in their daily existence hundreds of times every day. Lining up the world religions one next to the other on a chart and simply looking at what they believe, for example, what happens to a person when they die, the nature of salvation, the nature of the human soul, and the nature of God and man, will reveal irreconcilable differences between these religions. The undeniable fact remains that something is right and something is true regarding true spirituality and eternal life. We have put our trust in Jesus who proclaimed Himself as "the way, the truth, and the life" (John 14:6).

4) How do you explain all of the evil and suffering that is in the world? (Why do bad things happen to good people?)

This is one of the most difficult objections that non-Christians have towards the Gospel simply because of the logic of the following argument. "Either God is not good and loving because He allows evil to continue, or He is not all-powerful because He is unable to prevent it from occurring." A third alternative is possible: that is for God to create a truly significant universe, it was necessary for Him to create beings with free, moral choice. This renders the virtues of love, kindness, servanthood, and goodness to be real and significant in human relations. The other alternative seems to be for Him to create a universe of automatons that are simply led by the laws of cause and effect with God Himself being the only Cause. A world of robots or a world of significant human beings seem to be God's only two choices when He created the universe.

The plain teaching of Scripture is that all of the evil and most of the suffering in the world are the result of the sinful choices of selfish human beings and the influence of satanic powers of darkness that are just as real as God. This is self-evident even if we didn't have a Bible to refer to. The admittedly difficult questions of natural disasters, accidents, sicknesses, and diseases are simply the result of living in a fallen, imperfect world. While a non-Christian may not understand the concept of the "fallen-ness" of man that we understand as Christians (with our references to Genesis 3), we must again rely on the apparent "choices" that God had before Him to create a perfect universe. He could have made it "perfect" because He meticulously controlled everything, or He could have created a universe with an element of "chance" in which much of what happens was necessitated by the original sinful choices of the first man and was passed down to the rest of us.

5) If God knew man was going to sin before He created him, why did He go ahead with His plans?

The subject of God's foreknowledge and the questions that follow regarding His choosing people to be saved are thorny objections for the thinking skeptic. We must first explain to our non-Christian friends that we are by nature finite human beings with limited intellects trying to understand and explain the processes and thinking of an infinite, transcendent, eternal God. Therefore, we must proceed with caution.

While God does know the future, we must first of all defend His character against any accusations of Him being at best a bumbler and at worst a sadomasochist who created a universe that He knew would rebel against Him and therefore cause Himself pain! I like to give the following scenario when facing this question with a non-Christian: "Suppose a skeptic on his way to hell was to stand before God and point an accusatory finger in His face and say 'Why did You go ahead and create me if you knew I was going to rebel against You and perish?' God could simply respond, 'First of all, it was not My will that you perish (2 Peter 3:9, 1 Timothy 2:4), and I originally created you to have eternal life. I showed you My kindness to draw you to repentance (Romans 2:4), and you refused the love of the truth that could have saved you (2 Thessalonians 2: 10)."

"Secondly, while it is true that I knew some would rebel against Me and some would accept Me, why should I penalize those who would accept Me by not giving them the glories of My creation and eternal life just because you would reject Me?'"

While all illustrations break down and scenarios like the one above are limited, they do give us a little bit of insight into God's reasons for creating the Earth.

6) What about those who have never heard the Gospel?

At this writing, there are between two and a half to three billion people who have never heard the Gospel explained to them in an understandable way. It is estimated that 64 percent of all humans from 30 A.D. to the present are in this category. Most of them have never heard the name of Jesus Christ. Will they perish because they have never heard His name?

First of all, it must be pointed out that God has provided one way to salvation. Jesus Himself stated this emphatically (see John 14:6), and Peter the apostle made this clear by declaring "for there is no other name under heaven given among men by which we must be saved" (Acts 4:12). The first three chapters of Romans point out clearly that, whether we are religious, moral, reckless, or ignorant sinners, we nonetheless fall short of the glory of God and are thereby subject to death and separation from God (see Romans 3:23).

There are two major views held by Christians around the world on this sensitive subject. The first is what we might call the "exclusivist" view. That is the above facts of the New Testament Scriptures are clear: people must hear about Christ, and if they don't hear about Him, they perish, not because they haven't heard His name, but simply because they are sinners. Usually, however, the exclusivist view doesn't go over well when being explained to an honestly skeptical non-Christian regarding the destiny of the un-evangelized.

An alternative view is the "inclusivist" view, which is while maintaining that Christ is the only way and there is no salvation apart from Him, it could be possible for God to save some people (still on the merits of Christ's death) who have never heard the Gospel. This is based on several factors:

a) God is a just judge. Genesis 18:25 declares that "the Judge of all the earth will do what is right." We must first of all stand up for the goodness and justice of God and proceed from there.

b) It is demonstrated in the Old Testament that *before Christ*, many Old Testament saints were justified by their faith in God as they understood Him with the light that they had received. "And he believed in the LORD, and He accounted it to him for righteousness" (Genesis 15:6). Technically speaking, these Old Testament saints never heard the name of Jesus and yet were justified by their faith. The question is of course could this justification be possible after Christ?

c) Paul, in Romans 1 and 2, gives us four "lights" of God's revelation to man. The first two are what we call "general" revelation. That is the above-mentioned lights of creation and conscience. The second two lights are the "special" revelation of the Law and the Gospel. Could God with His absolute foreknowledge, absolute knowledge of the human heart, and absolute knowledge of what a person would have done if they had received the Gospel, judge a person according to how they had responded to the light they had received, whether it is general or special?

I realize that the inclusivist view does have problems and could perhaps dull the edge of our missionary thrust and take away its urgency. (John Piper has argued convincingly for this point in his book, *Let the Nations Be Glad! The Supremacy of God in Missions*.) We must also be careful not to go too far and thus open up the door so that people think they can be saved simply by being a good person. It may help, however, a skeptical non-Christian to rest easier that in the justice and goodness of God, He will judge righteously everyone upon the face of the earth whether they had received the light of the Gospel or not. Meanwhile, those of us that are involved in missionary work should not let up at all in our urgency to reach every person with the Gospel.

7) Why are there so many hypocrites in the church?

Unfortunately, there <u>are</u> many hypocrites in the church, and we must not make any excuses for those who say they are disciples of Jesus and yet in their lives deny Him. When a non-Christian skeptic makes this suggestion to me, I usually make the choice to "humble out" and admit that there are many hypocrites in the church.

First, without trying to make any excuses, I explain that the church is not a trophy case for perfect people, but a hospital for sinners. People come into the church broken and beaten up by sin and often are not changed overnight. Their destiny was changed by the One they have trusted in for their salvation (justification), but they have not yet entered into the total reality of being conformed to the image of Christ (sanctification). I then further explain that Christianity is not "all about" the Christians—whether or not they are hypocritical. It is "all about" Christ! Theoretically, if every Christian in the world was a hypocrite, it would not diminish the truth of who Jesus is and the fact that only He can save a human soul.

If someone tells me they wouldn't want to join a church because it has too many hypocrites, I may jokingly encourage them to come to church and add one more hypocrite to the number. Or I may suggest they come to church and help straighten out the rest of us hypocrites!

8) Isn't the Bible full of contradictions?

That the Bible is "full of contradictions" is an overstatement of the facts. There are some unexplainable minute errors that mostly have to do with discrepancies between numbers of people, for instance, in the Old Testament accounts of Kings and Chronicles. Most of these are minute both in detail and in importance, and they are most likely due to small errors by the copyists. After studying the Bible for 25 years, I am not aware of any contradictions in the Bible that would affect any of the major doctrines of Scripture regarding the nature of God, man, or salvation.

When someone asks me about the apparent contradictions in the Bible, I simply get out my Bible, hand it to them, and say, "Could you show me one, please?" Most of the people who have made such a dogmatic statement to me have not been able to point out one contradiction! This is because this objection is oftentimes a smokescreen from those who have heard someone else make that statement, and in an effort to sound intellectually secure, they have come down on the wrong side of the truth. In love, we need to point out that the Bible is not 1 book, but 66 books written by 40 different authors over a 1,600 year time span that deals with hundreds of controversial subjects without contradiction or error and with amazing unity, harmony, and accuracy.

9) Did Jesus rise from the dead?

The Bible freely admits that if Jesus did not rise from the dead, then Christianity is invalid. Paul even declared that without the resurrection, "…our preaching is useless, and so is your faith" (1 Corinthians 15:14, NIV). As mentioned in chapter 8, more than a few skeptics have sought to disprove the resurrection and became believers through the process. This was because they honestly examined the evidence. Below are a few pieces of evidence for the skeptic to consider before rendering a final verdict on the resurrection.

First, there is the account of Jesus' death. By analyzing the medical and historical data, Dr. Alexander Metherall, a physician who also has a doctorate in engineering, concluded that Jesus couldn't have survived the rigorous torture of crucifixion much less the gaping wound that pierced His lung and heart. In fact, He was in serious to critical condition before He even got to the cross as a result of the horrific flogging He received.

Secondly, we know from the Gospel accounts that the stone had been rolled away from the tomb. It is estimated that the stone would have weighed between one and a half to two tons. That Jesus would have been able to wake up in the dark tomb, push away the stone, and escape after the flogging and crucifixion would have been humanly impossible. There were 16 soldiers watching Jesus' body throughout that night, and all knew the Roman law that anyone caught deserting a night watch was deserving of death. Again, it is highly unlikely that even 1 guard would have left his post, but that all 16 would have left is unimaginable.

Thirdly, we have the evidence of the fact that Jesus' body has never been discovered and then the objective evidence of the existence of the Christian church and the martyrdom of all His disciples with the exception of John (Who would die for a lie?). This in addition to the celebration of church on Sunday in remembrance of His resurrection and the celebration of Easter are all evidences that point to the fact of the resurrection of Christ.

Oftentimes when skeptics question Christianity, they do it on the mistaken notion that Christ wasn't really risen from the dead, but oftentimes they have never looked at the evidence. A slow and painstaking delineation of such evidence will help open up your non-Christian friend's heart if he or she is willing to listen.

10) Why is Jesus the only way to God?

Jesus is the only way to God for at least three reasons.

Who He was. Jesus is not the only way to God because He gave us good teachings or performed miracles. Many others have done miracles and taught religious truth. Jesus is the only way to God because He was God Himself. This is what gives Him the authority to declare: "I am the way, the truth, and the life. No one comes to the Father except through Me" (John 14:6).

Through various sects of political and sociological circumstances, religious leaders like Mohammad, Siddhartha Gautama (Buddha), Confucius, and others have risen to prominence by their teachings, but none have claimed to be God. Jesus does not have authority because He gained a following, but because even in the virgin's womb, He was God in human flesh. This separates Him from all of the other religious leaders and consequently makes Him the only way to God.

What He said. Not only do Jesus' words have power just because they are intrinsic wisdom but because of Whom it was that uttered them. Because of Jesus' identity, His words carried the ultimate weight. He claimed to be the only way to God. He claimed to be God in the flesh, and He prophesied that He was going to rise from the dead. As author C.S. Lewis has aptly pointed out, Jesus said He was the Son of God, and if He was not and knew it, He was a *liar*. If He was not the Son of God and thought He was, He was a *lunatic*. But if He said He was the Son of God and He was, then we have no alternative but to accept Him as *Lord*, the only way to God.

What He did. Not only did Jesus give us the most profound teaching ever uttered by a human being, and not only did He perform miracles including raising others from the dead and then rising from the dead Himself, but He lived a sinless life.

Obviously, volumes could be written about each one of these ten subjects. My purpose here was not to exhaust the materials available to us to answer the questions of the skeptic. It was simply to give a "pop-apologetic" to the questions being asked by the folks in our culture regarding Christ. Appendix IV is given to whet your appetite for future study so that you can give, as Francis Schaeffer exhorted us, "Honest answers to honest questions."

APPENDIX II

Street Jesus
(Taking the Gospel to Where the People Are)

In the last few years, a plethora of books have been written related to the subject of lifestyle evangelism (including this one). Most of what has been shared in the main body of this book can be applied using these principles wherever you find yourself working, living, or playing. Those situations will present opportunities for "interest doors" through which we can walk with the Gospel.

In this appendix, however, I would like to deal with what some have termed "cold-contact" evangelism. Even though the word cold sounds "cold", I want to do my best to warm up a subject that is very dear to my heart—taking Jesus to the streets.

I was led to Christ because a total stranger walked up to me on the beach, offered me a Gospel newspaper, and lovingly asked for a few minutes of my time. My eternal destiny was changed as a result of that "cold-contact." While recognizing the statistics mentioned earlier in the book (the majority of people coming to Christ through personal "friendship" evangelism), I think there are many reasons for taking Jesus directly to the streets.

First, street evangelism is Biblical. Jesus sent His disciples out to preach the Gospel, first on a short-term outreach (Matthew 10 and Luke 9 and 10) and then on longer-term outreaches. On none of these occasions did He say "Go into all the world and earn your right to share the Gospel with people." He simply told us to go and preach.

The Book of Acts is full of people doing "cold-contact" evangelism. When Philip went down to the city of Samaria, there's no evidence that he had any previous contact with them. When Paul went on his various missionary journeys, it is obvious that he never met those people before. While using interest doors and being culturally sensitive, he went to total strangers and told them the good news of Jesus.

Secondly, street evangelism enables us to interact with the people you might not meet any other way. Recognizing that they need to be approached in a sensitive way (because we know most people are not out there waiting to get witnessed to), we must always be friendly and constantly remember that we represent Jesus.

Thirdly, street evangelism is good for us. It helps us to face the inevitable rejection, fear, and sometimes persecution that is promised to us in the New Testament (see 2 Timothy 3:12 and Matthew 5:10-12). Much teaching on evangelism tries to make the Gospel so user-friendly that it takes away the offense of the cross (see Galatians 5:11). When we go back to the Book of Acts, we see that apostles did not sugarcoat the message, but were lovingly confrontative in challenging people about their need to repent. Some evangelism equippers have even suggested that if we get into a situation in which people reject us and hate us that the Spirit must not be leading us. I actually find that getting rejected, spit on, threatened, and criticized is actually good for my soul! It enables me to enter into the sufferings of Christ and to feel the rejection that our Heavenly Father feels every day when He is rejected by millions of people who do not receive His good news. An insight can be gained from the early apostles who, when persecuted, "rejoiced that they were counted worthy to suffer shame for His name" (see Acts 5:40-42).

Lastly, street evangelism helps us to make friends with non-Christians. We must not allow ourselves to polarize between friendship evangelism and cold-contact evangelism as if they were enemies. The issue is whether or not we are reaching people with the Gospel. Obviously, building relationships with people and getting to know them is a good way of building a bridge so that we can share the Gospel with them. However, I have found a regular diet of going to the streets, passing out tracts, and just hanging out with non-Christians are good ways of building friendships. Surveys tell us that the average Christian does not have any non-Christian friends after two years of being saved. The many wonderful opportunities we have for Christian growth and fellowship can actually squeeze out of our schedule any time for friendships with non-Christians. If we take advantage of normal relational skills such as remembering people's names, where they work, and what things interest them, we can cultivate relationships and build up trust for friendship evangelism.

How to Witness on the Streets

How do we approach a total stranger on the street and start talking to him or her about Jesus? This is a dilemma that many Christians find themselves in when beginning street witnessing. To be honest, after 25 years of street evangelism, I have not found many suave, debonair ways of breaking into conversation about the most important Person in the universe with a total stranger. Usually there is a feeling of awkwardness on both your side and the side of the person who is receiving your approach. A pleasant, friendly, smiling approach oftentimes "breaks the ice" in the initial awkward seconds of a conversation. Try not to be too pushy at this point and put yourself in their shoes. Keep in mind that most people are not out on the street praying and waiting for someone to come up and tell them that they need to change their lives.

Initially I try not to give the impression that I am going to require an enormous amount of time out of the person I am approaching. I simply approach them usually with some type of Gospel tract, booklet, or invitation to a Christian event and ask them if I can have just a few minutes of their time. Responses vary, but they will more than likely mirror the following: they totally ignore you and pretend that you do not even exist (that is the toughest one to swallow!); they say "no" with varying degrees of hostility; or they look at you quizzically. When they look at you quizzically, chances are they have a thousand thoughts going through their mind including: "Is this person a cultist? What is this person's angle?" Or "What do they want from me? How much is it going to cost?" We must keep in mind that those types of concerns are natural and normal for a person to have, so in the first few seconds of a conversation, I try to keep in mind the need to help them relax. Often I approach a person with a smile and say "Can I give you something to read?" Or "Would you like some good news?" Or "Have you seen one of these yet?"

I have found that using a direct approach is the best way to witness on the street. If we are not open about our purpose, it usually backfires. Once I was beating around the bush with someone for 20 minutes, asking them about their job, their interests, their hobbies, and otherwise making senseless small talk. When I did turn the corner and bring up Jesus, they looked me in the eye, confronted me, and said, "Is that why you have been so friendly to me for the last couple of minutes because you wanted to get me in the mood to lay your religious trip on me?!" In great embarrassment, I had to admit that he had me.

The direct approach has a couple of advantages. If a person doesn't want to hear what you have to say, they can tell you right at the outset, and you don't waste their time. It also saves you time and may very well launch you into a divine appointment that God has providentially arranged for you. Just continue as a farmer or a fisherman would to look for ground that is soft or fish that are biting so that you can continue your witnessing experience.

Organizations like Campus Crusade for Christ and Evangelism Explosion have published various types of "opening door" questions or surveys that can be used to open up witnessing conversations. If you feel comfortable with such a tool, I would encourage you to use it.

In the first couple of minutes, I consciously attempt to get the other person to do most of the talking. I realize that depending on their culture and personality, I could probably get a real compliant person to sit and listen to me for a long period of time, but that doesn't mean that I am communicating the Gospel to them. I find that the best communication on a personal level comes when *dialogue* is established. Dialogue (two people in the conversation) is best in a witnessing situation. Preaching is always a monologue, but witnessing is a dialogue. This helps relax the situation and paves the way for meaningful exchange. Jesus, in the parable of the great feast, included an urgent appeal to the workers being sent out with the invitation, "Go out into the highways and hedges, and compel them to come in..." (Luke 14:23). Street witnessing is one way to do just that.

APPENDIX III

The Top Ten Overstatements
Made About Evangelism

1) **"Evangelism is for Evangelists."** Yes, evangelism is for evangelists, but it is not limited to this ministry gift. The word evangelist is mentioned only three times in the New Testament (Acts 21:8, Ephesians 4:11, & 2 Timothy 4:5). The first simply designates Philip as an evangelist, which includes the command to "equip the saints for the work of the ministry" (of evangelism). The third records Paul exhorting Timothy (who was not an evangelist) to do the work of an evangelist. Since Jesus declared that the coming of the Holy Spirit was to empower us to be His witnesses, it would follow that evangelism is for all believers (see Acts 1:8). Since the vast majority of people that come to Christ do not come through evangelists but through the rest of the "normal" folks, I would presume that the above is an overstatement.

2) **"Souls are won on our knees."** This statement presupposes that our primary responsibility in evangelism is to pray for the lost. Although I would be the last person to demean the essential place of prayer in the evangelistic process, we must remember that Jesus didn't say, "Go into all the world and pray," He said, "Go into all the world and preach..." (Mark 16:15). Souls are won by proclamation of the Gospel opening the way for the Holy Spirit to draw people to Himself (see John 6:44). Catherine Booth once said, "If you are praying for someone when God is telling you to preach to them, they will go to hell while you are praying for them." Prayer is not a substitute for preaching the Word, but a powerful and essential supplement to it.

3) **Don't witness unless you have a "word from the Lord."** It is optimum for every Christian to be led by the Holy Spirit in all things, but we must keep in mind that the 66 books in the Bible are also a "word from the Lord." With regard to the primary commandments of Scripture (i.e., to love one another, love God, pray, etc.), we do not need to have a word from the Lord, but we simply need to do it. I am not advocating an indiscriminate approach to witnessing, but I am saying that a word from the Lord about witnessing has already been given to us (see Mark 16:15).

4) **We shouldn't witness unless we are moving in the "miraculous."** Some in the Signs-and-Wonders movement have advocated this theory, and certainly there is great impact when signs and wonders accompany the preaching of the Gospel (see Hebrews 2:4). However, we must never forget that the Gospel itself is the power of God unto salvation (see Romans 1:16). I believe that we cannot only "pray the power down," but I believe we can "preach the power down." Even if we are not experiencing miraculous signs, we should use the powerful words of the Gospel to give hope to people who desperately need to hear about Jesus.

5) **"You don't need to defend the truth. The truth defends itself."** Paul the apostle, who is certainly one of the foremost believers in the power of the truth, also taught and demonstrated that the Gospel at times needs to be defended. Jude told us to earnestly contend for the faith (see Jude 3) and Paul told the Philippians "I am appointed for the defense of the gospel" (Philippians 1:17). Peter commanded us to "always be ready to give a defense to everyone who asks you a reason for the hope that is in you" (1 Peter 3:15). The Book of Acts describes it as Paul's "custom" to reason with people in the synagogues from the Scriptures (see Acts 17:2). Apologists throughout church

history have defended the faith against intellectual attacks and perversions of the Gospel's truth for the last 2000 years. When the Gospel is under attack, it needs to be defended. Hence, the need for us to give honest answers to honest questions.

6) **"Just live a holy life and people will ask what you have that they don't."** People who make this statement love to quote St. Francis of Assisi when he said "go into all the world and preach the Gospel. Use words if necessary." This is a nice saying, but it is not exactly Biblical! Jesus does want us to let our light shine, but He never said people would run to us and ask what we have. He said we are to go and tell people the good news of the Gospel. The command of Christ is to preach the Gospel to lost people.

7) **"If we build it, they will come."** This statement comes from the movie "Field of Dreams," rather than the Bible. Yet, some believe that if we can just arrange our church services to cater to the un-churched people, they will come in and join the church. I am all for being as culturally relevant as we can be to reach lost people, but the way people have always gotten saved is by being confronted with their sin by the convicting work of the Holy Spirit. Christ's goodness allows them to see their need for forgiveness and to believe on Christ for their salvation. If a building helps us with these ends, so be it, but it is a supplement to the preaching of the Gospel, not a substitute for it.

8) **"We must work to change society, then the world will see that we have the answer."** Neither the Bible nor church history bears out this statement. Historical revivals have usually begun among the poor and worked their way up to change society. This was true in the early Roman Empire as well as in the

Great Awakenings in America. While it is true that we should work hard to be the salt of the earth, we must also be aware of the temptations to power which seem to be as Jesus said, "the Gentile way" of exercising Christ's lordship (see Matthew 20:25-26). If the religious right could have saved America, it would have been saved long ago.

9) **"We are living in a post-Christian era. People don't want to listen."** It is true that the typical young person growing up in the Western world is Biblically illiterate and that the Christian consensus has been lost as well. This, however, does not negate the absolute truth that all of mankind has a "God-shaped blank on the inside," as Blaise Pascal termed it. The fact that "creation was subjected to frustration" (see Romans 8:20) is true for all eras regardless of the worldview of that particular culture. To reach our generation, we must communicate the Gospel in such a way that people hear and understand it.

10) **"Gospel literature is impersonal and therefore doesn't work."** The great evangelist D.L. Moody was once criticized for his methods of sharing the Gospel, and his reply to the rather unfruitful person who was doing the criticizing was, "I like the way I am doing it better than the way you are not doing it!" I would say the same for the use of Gospel literature. For 25 years, I have consistently seen people come to Christ through the use of various types of Gospel tracts and books. While it is true that people are the best "epistles" for people to read (see 2 Corinthians 3:1-3), the printed page can be a wonderful supplement to our witnessing. Often Gospel tracts or Christian books will give us an opening to share with people about Jesus Christ. While standing alone, tracts may appear impersonal and programmatic, but they can be powerful tools for personal evangelism.

APPENDIX IV

Recommended Reading

Evangelism

1) *The Master Plan of Evangelism (Abridged)*, Robert E. Coleman, Fleming H. Revell Co.
2) *The Soul Winner*, Charles H. Spurgeon, Various Publishers
3) *A Passion for Souls: The Life of D.L. Moody*, Lyle W. Dorsett, Moody Press
4) *How to Give Away Your Faith (With Study Guide)*, Paul Little, Intervarsity Press
5) *Witnessing Without Fear*, Bill Bright, Thomas Nelson
6) *Harvest*, Chuck Smith, Word For Today
7) *How to Share Your Faith*, Greg Laurie, Tyndale House
8) *We Cannot But Tell*, Ross Tooley, YWAM Publishing
9) *Out of the Saltshaker & into the World*, Rebecca Pippert, Intervarsity Press
10) *Living Proof*, Jim Petersen, Navpress

Missions

1) *Peace Child*, Don Richardson, Gospel Light Publishing
2) *Bruchko*, Bruce Olson, Creation House
3) *Let the Nations Be Glad*, John Piper, Baker Book House
4) *The Church is Bigger Than You Think*, Patrick Johnstone, Christian Focus Publications or the William Carey Library
5) *World Christian Encyclopedia*, David Barrett, Todd Johnson, George Kurian, Oxford University Press

6) *Is That Really You, God?* Loren Cunningham, YWAM Publishing

7) *Concise History of the Christian World Mission*, J. Herbert Kane, Baker Book House

8) *Perspectives on the World Christian Movement*, Ralph Winter, Steven Hawthorne, William Carey Library

9) *Eternity In Their Hearts*, Don Richardson, Gospel Light Publishing

10) *Operation World*, Patrick Johnstone & Jason Mandryk, Bethany House

Apologetics

1) *The Case for Christ*, Lee Strobel, Zondervan Publishing House

2) *The Case for Faith*, Lee Strobel, Zondervan Publishing House

3) *Can Man Live Without God*, Ravi Zacharias, W Publishing Group

4) *More Than A Carpenter*, Josh McDowell, Tyndale House

5) *The Testimony of the Evangelists*, Simon Greenleaf, Kregel Publications

6) *A Reasonable Faith*, William Lane Craig, Crossway Books

7) *Mere Christianity*, C.S. Lewis, Harper San Francisco

8) *Baker Encyclopedia of Christian Apologetics*, Norman Geisler, Baker Book House

9) *The Face That Demonstrates the Farce of Evolution*, Hank Hanegraaff, W Publishing Group

10) *The Natural Sciences Know Nothing of Evolution*, A.E. Wilder-Smith, The Word For Today

100 Reasons We Should Evangelize the World

1) God loves people (John 3:16 ♦ Romans 5:8).

2) Jesus died for sinners (1 Corinthians 15:3).

3) Jesus commanded us to go (Mark 16:15).

4) The Gospel is true (1 Corinthians 15:1-4).

5) There is "no other name" that can save (Acts 4:12).

6) God is not willing that any should perish (2 Peter 3:9).

7) Jesus came to seek and save the lost (Matthew 18:11).

8) It's God's desire that all be saved (1 Timothy 2:4).

9) Jesus is a friend of sinners (Matthew 11:19).

10) Jesus rose from the dead (Romans 1:4 ♦ 1 Corinthians 15: 20).

11) God's heart is "broken" over sin (Ezekiel 6:9).

12) There is more value in a human soul than the whole world (Matthew 16:26).

13) Witnessing makes our feet "beautiful" (Isaiah 52:7 ♦ Romans 10:15).

14) God commands all men everywhere to repent (Acts 17:30).

15) Jesus came to reach the lost. We should follow His example (John 20:21).

16) The Bible is God's Word (2 Timothy 3:15-17).

17) God wants heaven populated with every tribe, language, and nation (Revelation 5:9, 7:9).

18) Jesus came to destroy the works of the devil (1 John 3:8).

19) Over two billion people have never heard the name of Jesus (Romans 15:20-21).

20) Jesus prayed for workers for the harvest (Matthew 9:37-38).

21) Witnessing for Christ was the purpose of Pentecost (Acts 1: 8).

22) Jesus is the source of life (John 14:6).

23) Heaven is real (Colossians 1:5).

24) Hell is hot (Revelation 20:15).

25) Soul winners "shine like the stars" (Daniel 12:3).

26) Soul winning brings joy to our lives (Psalm 126:5-6 ♦ 1 Thessalonians 2:19).

27) Jesus is the truth (John 14:6).

28) Faith in Jesus pleases God (Hebrews 11:6).

29) Satan has blinded the minds of non-believers (2 Corinthians 4:4).

30) We can receive a "soul winners' crown" (1 Thessalonians 2: 19).

31) The Gospel is the power of God unto salvation (Romans 1: 16).

32) Witnessing is our debt to the nations (Romans 1:14).

33) The preaching of the cross is the power of God (1 Corinthians 1:18).

34) Evangelism helps fulfill God's "eternal purpose" (Ephesians 1:9-11, 3:9-11).

35) It is more blessed to give than to receive (Acts 20:35).

36) We are ambassadors for Christ (2 Corinthians 5:20).

37) Hell is dark (Jude 13).

38) The world needs answers (1 Peter 3:15).

39) Many false prophets and cults are deceiving people (Matthew 24:5,11,24).

40) Gospel work is never in vain (1 Corinthians 15:58).

41) God promised to fill the earth with His glory (Numbers 14: 21 ♦ Habakkuk 2:14).

42) One billion Muslims—Jesus is the one true God in the flesh (Colossians 2:9).

43) God's promises are for every generation (Acts 2:39).

44) Every person must face God's judgment (Hebrews 9:27).

45) The Gospel reveals the righteousness of God (Romans 1:17).

46) Jesus is the truth (John 14:6).

47) Witnessing helps fulfill God's covenant w/Abraham (Genesis 12:1-3 ♦ Galatians 3:8).

48) Hell is forever (Matthew 25:46).

49) Jesus is coming back again (Revelation 22:12).

50) Gospel work builds unity in the body of Christ (Philippians 1:27).

51) God longs to be a father to everyone (2 Corinthians 6:17-18 ♦ Galatians 3:26).

52) Spreading the Gospel helps provoke Israel to jealousy (Romans 11:11).

53) Gospel preaching "manifests" (brings to life, NIV) God's Word (Titus 1:3).

54) Christ has redeemed us from the curse of the Law (Galatians 3:13).

55) We are living in the last days (Hebrews 1:2).

56) 800 million Hindus—Jesus died for all (1 John 2:2).

57) Jesus told us to make disciples of all nations (Matthew 28:18-20).

58) The world will shortly be burned up (2 Peter 3:10).

59) God desires "the obedience of faith" among all nations (Romans 1:5, 16:26).

60) Faith comes by hearing God's Word (Romans 10:17).

61) The world cannot hear without "preachers" (Romans 10:14).

62) Witnessing helps fulfill the Lord's Prayer, "Thy kingdom come" (Matthew 6:10).

63) Jesus told us to go to the "uttermost parts of the earth" (Acts 1:8).

64) God is able to save to the "uttermost" (Hebrews 7:25).

65) God promised to pour out His Spirit on all mankind in the last days (Acts 2:17).

66) God has declared Himself in the creation. We need to do "follow-up" (Psalm 19:1-4 ♦ Romans 1:20, 10:18).

67) Evangelism keeps us from worldliness (the "good news shoes" keep us clean) (Ephesians 6:15).

68) God has opened doors for the Gospel all over the world (1 Corinthians 16:9).

69) Jesus came to "cast fire on the earth." We should keep it blazing (Luke 12:49).

70) "We believe, therefore we speak" (2 Corinthians 4:13).

71) "Let the redeemed of the Lord say so" (Psalm 107:2).

72) All believers are priests—we should represent God to the nations (1 Peter 2:5-9 ♦ Revelation 5:9-10).

73) Jesus had compassion on the multitudes. So should we (Matthew 9:36).

74) 250 million tribal peoples. God has placed eternity in their hearts (Ecclesiastes 3:11).

75) God's blessing is for all nations (Psalm 67:1-2).

76) The nations are our inheritance (Psalm 2:8).

77) We can deliver people from this "present evil age" (Galatians 1:4).

78) One billion Chinese people (God must love the Chinese— He made so many of them!) (Revelation 7:9).

79) David served God's purpose in his generation. So should we (Acts 13:36).

80) God told us to declare His glory among the nations and His wonders to all people (Psalm 96:3).

81) God "swore" He would bless all nations (Genesis 22:16-17 ♦ Hebrews 6:12-16).

82) Witnessing helps us experience rejection and thereby makes us more like Jesus (Isaiah 53:3).

83) There is a new world coming (2 Peter 3:13).

84) The Gospel gives people righteousness, peace, and joy (Romans 14:17).

85) One billion people live in abject poverty worldwide. Jesus preached to the poor. So should we (Luke 4:18).

86) God created the universe; He deserves our worship (Genesis 1:1).

87) Soul winning reduces the amount of sin in the world (James 5:20).

88) Jesus came to "bear witness to the truth." So should we (John 18:37).

89) World evangelization was Paul's "apostolic ambition." It should be ours (Romans 1:5, 15:20).

90) Paul became "all things to all men" in order to save the lost. So should we (1 Corinthians 9:20-22).

91) We are called to be "fellow-workers with God" (1 Corinthians 3:9 ♦ 2 Corinthians 6:1).

92) The Gospel has been given to us as a "trust" (1 Timothy 1:11).

93) People without Christ are lost, having "no hope and without God in the world" (Ephesians 2:12).

94) Jesus came to set the captives free (Luke 4:18).

95) People are created with an emptiness only God can fill (Romans 8:20).

96) We are under "obligation" to witness for Jesus (Romans 1:14).

97) God has a plan, a destiny for everyone's life (Ephesians 2:10).

98) Jesus came to give "abundant life" (John 10:10).

99) The "word of faith is near" to everyone who calls on the Lord (Romans 10:8-10).

100) "NOW IS THE DAY OF SALVATION!" (2 Corinthians 6:2).

ENDNOTES

Section I
[1] C.H. Spurgeon, *The Soul Winner*, Eerdmans, 1964, pg. 15.
[2] Elmer Towns, *Church Growth: State of the Art*, Tyndale, 1986, pg. 53.
[3] Dr. D. James Kennedy, *Evangelism Explosion Manual*, Tyndale, 1993, pg. 4.
[4] Loren Cunningham, *Winning God's Way*, YWAM Publishing, 1988, pgs. 89-92.

Chapter 2
[5] Bill Bright, Quoted in *The Calling of the Evangelist*, Worldwide Publications, 1986, pg. 27.

Chapter 4
[6] Earle E. Cairns, *Christianity Through the Centuries*, Zondervan, 1954, 1967, pg. 22.

Chapter 7
[7] Dietrich Bonhoeffer, *The Cost of Discipleship*, Simon & Schuster Trade Paperbacks, May 1976, pgs. 47-48.
[8] Chuck Colson, *Kingdoms in Conflict*, Zondervan, 1987, pg. 262.

Chapter 8
[9] Josh McDowell, *More Than a Carpenter*, Living Books, 1977, pg. 26.
[10] Josh McDowell, *More Than a Carpenter*, Living Books, 1977, pg. 89.
[11] Josh McDowell, *More Than a Carpenter*, Living Books, 1977, pg. 97.
[12] Josh McDowell, *More Than a Carpenter*, Living Books, 1977, pg. 98.
[13] Lee Strobel, *The Case for Christ*, Zondervan, 1998, pgs. 191-257.

Chapter 9
[14] George Barna, *Evangelism That Works*, Regal Books, 1995, pgs. 35-37.
[15] John Stott, *Christian Mission in the Modern World*, Falcon Press, 1975, pg. 54

Chapter 10
[16] James Hewitt, Editor, *Illustrations Unlimited*, Tyndale, 1988, pg. 175.
[17] Keith Green, *The Prodigal Son*, Sparrow Records, 1983.
[18] Howard Snyder, *The Radical Wesley*, Intervarsity Press, 1980, pg. 21.

Chapter 11
[19] Matthew Yi, *Associated Press*, 2000.

Chapter 12
[20] Robert Coleman, *The Master Plan of Evangelism*, Revell Press, 1979, pg. 11.
[21] Keith Green, *Jesus Commands Us to Go*, Jesus Commands Us to Go, Sparrow Records, 1984.

Chapter 13
[22] Jon Braun, *Whatever Happened to Hell?*, Thomas Nelson, 1979, pg. 86; Harold T. Bryson, *The Reality of Hell and the Goodness of God*, Tyndale, 1984, pg. 44.
[23] Jonathan Edwards (sermon), *Sinners in the Hands of an Angry God*, Enfield, Connecticut, 1741.
[24] Leonard Ravenhill, *Why Revival Tarries*, Bethany House, 1983, pg. 32.

Chapter 14
[25] Michael Green, *Evangelism in the Early Church*, Eerdmans, 1970, pgs. 266-269.
[26] Patrick Johnstone, *The Church is Bigger Than You Think*, William Carey Library, 1998, pgs. 109-116.
[27] Robert Coleman, *The Coming World Revival*, Crossway Books, 1995, pg. 159.

Chapter 15
[28] Bill Bright, *Four Spiritual Laws*, Campus Crusade for Christ, 1965, 1995.
[29] Quoted in Ruth Tucker, *From Jerusalem to Irian Jaya*, Zondervan, 1983, pg. 241.
[30] Richard Collier, *The General Next to God*, Fontana, 1965, pg. 190.
[31] From a personal conversation with Don Stephens.

Section IV
[32] W. Charles Arn, *Church Growth: State of the Art*, Tyndale, 1986, pg. 60.

Chapter 16
[33] Audio tape by Dr. Mark Eastman, *The Creator and Cosmos*, Genesis Outreach, 1995.

[34] Lee Strobel, *The Case for Christ*, Zondervan, 1998, pgs. 103-118.
[35] Ibid. pg. 81.
[36] Norman Geisler and William Nix, *General Introduction to the Bible*, Moody Press, 1986, pg. 367.

Chapter 17
[37] C. Peter Wagner, *Church Planting for a Greater Harvest*, Regal Press, 1971, pg. 12.

Chapter 18
[38] Quoted in *The Work of an Evangelist*, Worldwide Publications, 1994, pg. 23.
[39] J. Gilchrist Lawson, *Deeper Experiences of Famous Christians*, Whitaker House, 1998, pg. 237.

Chapter 20
[40] George Peters, *Saturation Evangelism*, Zondervan, 1979, pgs. 72-81.
[41] Robert Coleman, *The Master Plan of Evangelism*, Revell Press, 1979, pg. 11.
[42] Sidney Diamond, *the Psychology of the Methodist Revival*, Oxford Press, 1926, pg. 112.
[43] Howard Snyder, *The Radical Wesley*, Intervarsity Press, 1980, pg. 147.